# NBA LEGENDS

**The word legend is thrown around all too readily these days, but there can be no doubt that the NBA players featured in this book are the very best to have ever graced a basketball court. They are true legends of the game.**

Spanning the decades and covering all the league's most iconic eras, we uncover the fascinating stories and incredible accomplishments of the greatest basketball players of all time, from the game's first superstars, Wilt Chamberlain, Bill Russell and Jerry West, to the modern-day greats of the late Kobe Bryant, LeBron James and Kevin Garnett. There are also in-depth features on Lakers legends Magic Johnson, Kareem Abdul-Jabbar and Shaquille O'Neal, as well as Celtics great Larry Bird, while we also explore 23 reasons why Michael Jordan is *the* greatest of all time.

It's not just about great players, though. Without great coaches there would be no great players, legendary teams or memorable matchups. That's why we also run down the ten most successful and influential coaches from NBA history, look back at the ten greatest championship-winning teams and relive ten of the best games of all time. But we kick things off with a collection of the 50 most iconic NBA players the world has ever seen. Enjoy!

First published in the UK 2020 by Sona Books
an imprint of Danann Publishing Ltd.

**WARNING:** For private domestic use only, any unauthorised Copying,
hiring, lending or public performance of this book is illegal.

Published under licence from Future Publishing Limited a Future PLC group company. All rights reserved. No part of this publication may be reproduced or stored in a retrieval system or transmitted in any form or by any means without the prior written permission of the publisher.

© 2018 Future Publishing PLC

All Images courtesy of Getty Images, except;
Getty Images
Wiki © Fred Palumbo P72
Getty Images/Vernon Biever P82
Wiki © Keith Allison P103
Wiki © Vernon J. Biever P122

CAT NO: SON0479
ISBN: 978-1-912918-31-7

Made in EU.

# CONTENTS

- 12   50 ICONIC NBA PLAYERS
- 28   KOBE BRYANT
- 36   JERRY WEST
- 38   LARRY BIRD
- 44   SHAQUILLE O'NEAL
- 50   10 OF THE GREATEST COACHES
- 58   MICHAEL JORDAN
- 68   HAKEEM OLAJUWON
- 72   WILT CHAMBERLAIN
- 76   JULIUS ERVING
- 78   KAREEM ABDUL-JABBAR

- 84   10 GREATEST NBA GAMES
- 92   MAGIC JOHNSON
- 98   LEBRON JAMES
- 104   DAVID ROBINSON
- 106   DIRK NOWITZKI
- 110   BILL RUSSELL
- 112   TIM DUNCAN
- 116   JOHN STOCKTON
- 118   TOP 10 LEGENDARY TEAMS
- 126   KEVIN GARNETT
- 128   KARL MALONE

NBA LEGENDS

# 50 ICONIC NBA PLAYERS

**DEFINING THE LEAGUE'S MANY ERAS, THESE ARE THE 50 ICONS WHO MADE THE NBA WHAT IT IS TODAY…**

It's impossible to write a definitive list of the 50 greatest players in NBA history. Measuring an MVP from the 1950s against the achievements of a great player in today's league is a futile task; the game of basketball has changed and evolved so dramatically throughout the NBA's long and illustrious history.

Instead, what we have here is a list of 50 NBA icons, all of whom made an indelible mark on the league in some way or another. Each of the players here has left a legacy that endures today, be it through amazing statistical achievements, unquestioned leadership and winning mentality, extraordinary endurance or, more often than not, all of the above. From George Mikan – the league's first superstar – to stars of today like LeBron James and Steph Curry, this list spans the full seven decades of the NBA, every position on the court and most of its teams represented.

## GEORGE MIKAN

**01** Mikan was the NBA's first superstar, leading the Minneapolis Lakers to five titles in six years from 1948 to 1954.

He led the league in scoring three times and rebounding twice. He suffered ten broken bones throughout his career, which led to an early retirement in 1956. Still, he was inducted into the Hall of Fame in 1959.

George Mikan: all this and playing in specs too!

Elgin Baylor: early 1960s supremo

## ELGIN BAYLOR

**02** Small forward Baylor spent a long time in the shadow of Wilt Chamberlain and Bill Russell, but the Lakers icon was a legend in his own right.

He topped 34 points per game for three straight seasons from 1961-63. The ten-time 1st All-NBA team legend finished his career with 27.4 points and 13.5 rebounds per game, but never won the title.

## STEVE NASH

**03** Two-time MVP Nash is one of the 21st century's greatest point guards, despite never winning the title.

He led the league in assists per game five times while playing for Phoenix, ranking third in career assists. Nash is the most accurate free throw shooter in NBA history at .904 for his career.

## JASON KIDD

**04** An incredibly versatile point guard, Kidd led the league in assists five times between 1999 and 2004, while topping seven rebounds per game six times in his 19 seasons in the league.

After two appearances in the finals with the Nets, the 12-time All-Star finally won the title with Dallas in 2011.

## CHRIS PAUL

**05** Widely considered the best point guard still playing, Paul is still looking for his first title.

Despite leading the NBA in assists four times and steals six times, he still hasn't tasted much postseason success. After two years as the floor general for the fearsome Houston Rockets superteam, in 2019 he moved to the Oklahoma City Thunder in search of that elusive first NBA championship.

# NBA LEGENDS

## KOBE BRYANT

**06** Ask any Lakers fan, and they will confidently tell you that Kobe was the greatest of all time.

In his prime, KB led the Lakers to five titles as an unstoppable offensive force, while also being one of the NBA's foremost perimeter defenders. Winning an MVP award, he made the All-NBA First Team 11 times and the All-Defensive First Team nine times, twice leading the league in points per game. After 20 years with the Lakers he bowed out as the third highest scorer in NBA history. He was tragically killed in a helicopter crash in January 2020.

## MOSES MALONE

**07** Often forgotten when it comes to the conversation of the greatest centers in NBA history, Malone was nothing short of a force of nature during his prime in the 1980s.

He came straight out of high school into the ABA in 1974, and in 1976 he entered the NBA and immediately started dominating. His years with Houston and Philadelphia were especially illustrious, where he was named MVP in 1979, 1982 and 1983. He led the league in rebounding six times from 1979 to 1985, including a title season with the 76ers in 1983, where he was selected Finals MVP. He appeared in 12 straight All-Star games from 1978 to 1989. Since the NBA started counting offensive rebounds, nobody has yet outdone Malone's career tally of 6,731.

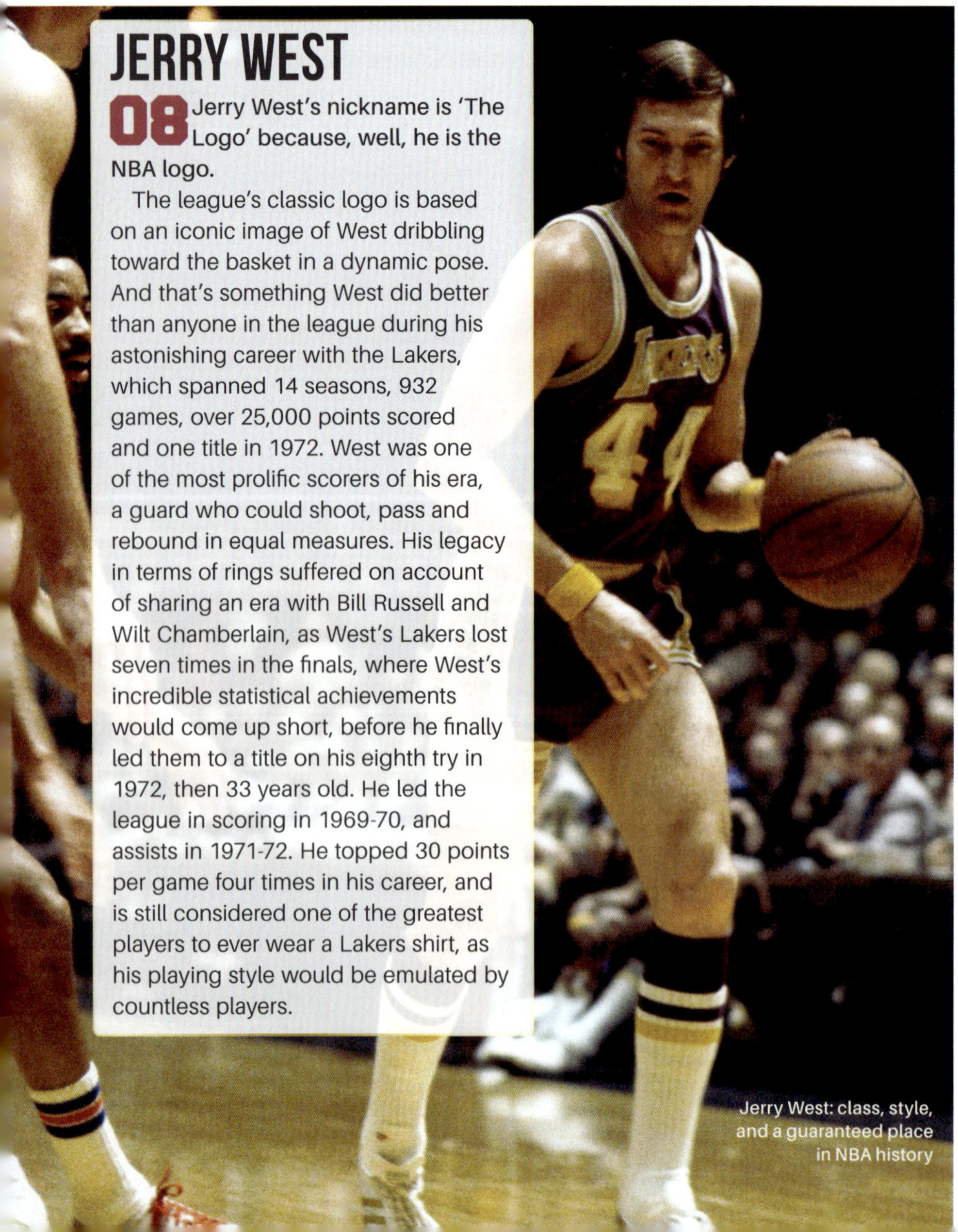

## JERRY WEST

**08** Jerry West's nickname is 'The Logo' because, well, he is the NBA logo.

The league's classic logo is based on an iconic image of West dribbling toward the basket in a dynamic pose. And that's something West did better than anyone in the league during his astonishing career with the Lakers, which spanned 14 seasons, 932 games, over 25,000 points scored and one title in 1972. West was one of the most prolific scorers of his era, a guard who could shoot, pass and rebound in equal measures. His legacy in terms of rings suffered on account of sharing an era with Bill Russell and Wilt Chamberlain, as West's Lakers lost seven times in the finals, where West's incredible statistical achievements would come up short, before he finally led them to a title on his eighth try in 1972, then 33 years old. He led the league in scoring in 1969-70, and assists in 1971-72. He topped 30 points per game four times in his career, and is still considered one of the greatest players to ever wear a Lakers shirt, as his playing style would be emulated by countless players.

*Jerry West: class, style, and a guaranteed place in NBA history*

## KEVIN GARNETT

**09** One of the most colourful and passionate players of the last two decades, 'KG' suffered from playing on the talent-depleted Minnesota Timberwolves for much of his career.

A great offensive player, Garnett was named the 2004 MVP, and also led the league in rebounding four years in a row from 2004 to 2007 before sacrificing individual stats for team success, when he joined the Celtics. And that's where his legacy was made. In 2008, he led them to their first title in 22 years. It would be his only title, but this future Hall of Famer still had a glittering career. Only five players have ever played more than his 1,462 games, and he's the NBA's ninth most prolific rebounder, with 14,662 over his career.

# 50 ICONIC NBA PLAYERS

## WILT CHAMBERLAIN

**10** Chamberlain holds several NBA records that will probably never be broken.

Among those are his incredible 1961-62 season where he averaged 50.4 points and 25.7 rebounds per game, his career rebounding average of 22.9, and of course his historic 100-point game. He was quite simply the most dominant player in NBA history. A modern, athletic 7' 1" center, so talented he could be an MVP contender even in today's era of hyper-physical fitness, but playing in the 1960s there was only one player who could even remotely keep up with him. Fatefully, it was this player, Bill Russell, who would prevent Wilt from ever winning more than two titles. He led the league in scoring seven times, rebounding 11 times and even managed a season where he averaged 48.5 minutes per game, despite a regulation NBA game only lasting 48 minutes. Only Michael Jordan averaged more than Wilt's 30.1 points per game over his career.

## OSCAR ROBERTSON

**11** It's considered an achievement in the NBA to record a triple-double. For Oscar Robertson, however, it was just part of his job.

He was the first player to average a triple-double over a season, when he tallied 30.8 points, 12.5 rebounds and 11.4 assists per game in 1961-62. In fact, he averaged a triple-double over his first five combined seasons, leading the NBA in assists per game for four of those. The 1963-64 MVP finally won the title in 1971 when he signed with the Milwaukee Bucks from the Cincinnati Royals. Robertson is still considered the gold standard when it comes to stat-stuffing point guards.

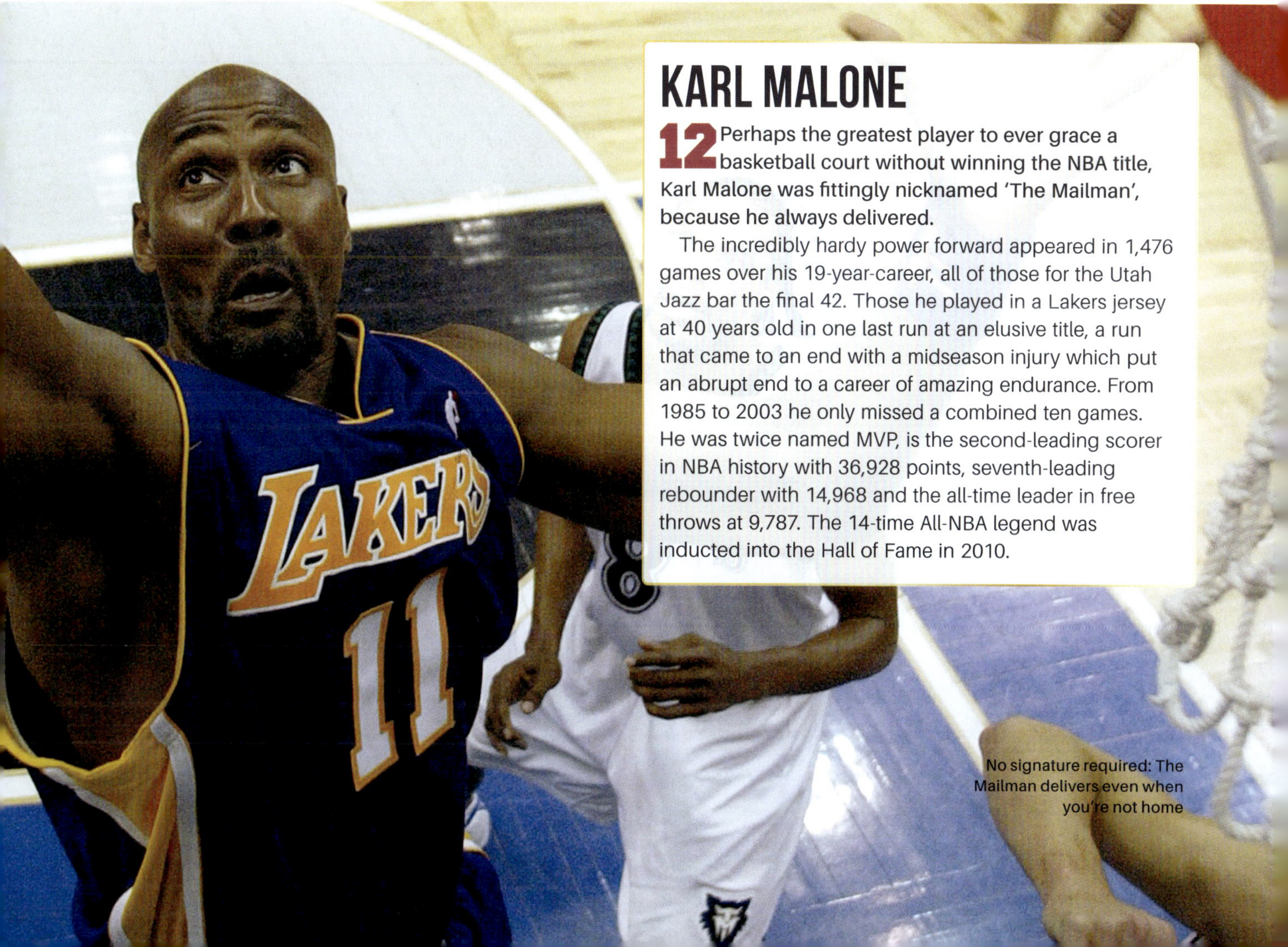

## KARL MALONE

**12** Perhaps the greatest player to ever grace a basketball court without winning the NBA title, Karl Malone was fittingly nicknamed 'The Mailman', because he always delivered.

The incredibly hardy power forward appeared in 1,476 games over his 19-year-career, all of those for the Utah Jazz bar the final 42. Those he played in a Lakers jersey at 40 years old in one last run at an elusive title, a run that came to an end with a midseason injury which put an abrupt end to a career of amazing endurance. From 1985 to 2003 he only missed a combined ten games. He was twice named MVP, is the second-leading scorer in NBA history with 36,928 points, seventh-leading rebounder with 14,968 and the all-time leader in free throws at 9,787. The 14-time All-NBA legend was inducted into the Hall of Fame in 2010.

*No signature required: The Mailman delivers even when you're not home*

# NBA LEGENDS

## HAKEEM OLAJUWON

**13** Hakeem 'The Dream' is one of the greatest centers in NBA history, basically reinventing the position from the moment he entered the league in 1984.

A ferocious defender and the best shot-blocker in the modern NBA, Olajuwon was also a great offensive player, topping 20 points per game for every one of his first 13 seasons, while proving to be a good passer too. Hakeem led the league in blocks three times, and rebounding twice. After spending years in Michael Jordan's shadow, Olajuwon emerged as the league's new poster boy in 1993-94, when he was selected MVP and led the Houston Rockets to the first of two straight titles. Named Finals MVP in both 1994 and 1995, he was Defensive Player of the Year in 1993 and 1994 as well, and still leads the NBA in career blocks at 3,830.

Hanging tough: shot block maestro Hakeem

Taking aim: The Shaq about to sink another

## SHAQUILLE O'NEAL

**14** If Wilt Chamberlain was the most dominant player of the NBA's early era, Shaquille O'Neal surely holds that honour for the modern era.

Towering over most of the competition at 7' 1", he quickly added a lot of muscle after looking relatively gangly as a rookie. He was an instant All-Star in Orlando playing for the Magic, but his pursuit of league glory led him to sign with the Lakers in 1996, where he teamed up with Kobe Bryant to win three straight titles in 2000, 2001 and 2002, forming the first dynasty of the new millennium. He was named Finals MVP all three years, adding to his 2000 regular season MVP award, which would oddly enough be the only one in his career. He won a fourth title with the Miami Heat in 2006, then playing more of a supporting role to Dwyane Wade. Shaq's list of other accolades is a lengthy one, and includes two scoring titles in 1995 and 2000, as well as 15 All-Star games, eight All-NBA first team selections, and the eighth place on the NBA's all-time list for both points scored and shots blocked. In addition, O'Neal led the league in Player Efficiency Rating five times from 1997 to 2002, and his career Player Efficiency Rating (PER) of 26.4 ranks third all-time, behind only Michael Jordan and LeBron James.

## DIRK NOWITZKI

**15** Considered by many the greatest European in NBA history, Dirk Nowitzki made an indelible mark on the league over his 21-year career for the Dallas Mavericks.

A great three-point shooter, especially for a seven-foot-tall power forward, the 2007 MVP and 13-time All-Star delivered the Mavs their first-ever NBA title in 2011, named Finals MVP in the process. He retired in 2019 as the first and only player to remain with the same NBA team for 21 seasons and also the only player to pick up at least 31,000 points, 10,000 rebounds, 3,000 assists, 1,000 steals, 1,000 blocks and 1,000 two-point field goals in NBA history.

No one has played longer for the same team than Dirk Nowitzki has for the Dallas Mavericks

# 50 ICONIC NBA PLAYERS

17

Befitting an ABA legend, Dr J was one of the most prolific and creative dunkers of his era

## JULIUS ERVING

**16** The best player to emerge from the high-flying but short-lived ABA, Julius 'Dr J' Erving joined the Philadelphia 76ers in 1976 after leading the ABA in scoring three times, winning two titles with the New York Americans.

Although he never repeated that achievement in the NBA, he still became one of the league's biggest stars during the 1980s, winning the MVP award in 1981 and helping lead the Sixers to the title in 1983. Known for his talent at both ends of the court, Erving averaged 28.7 points, 12.1 rebounds, 4.8 assists, 2.4 steals and 2.0 blocks per game in his five seasons in the ABA, and 22.0 points, 6.7 rebounds, 3.9 assists, 1.8 steals and 1.5 blocks per game in 836 NBA games after that.

## STEPHEN CURRY

**17** Steph Curry has almost single-handedly forced the entire NBA to rethink their tactics in the last few years.

Curry emerged in 2012-13 as simply the greatest long-distance shooter the league has ever seen. The two-time MVP and three-time champion set a record in 2015-16 when he hit an absurd 5.1 three-pointers per game, leading the league in scoring that year with 30.1 points. He can easily hit shots all the way back to the centre circle, has great handles to take defenders on, is a good rebounder and great passer, and will be the poster boy for the new-era NBA for quite a few years yet.

Jordan has the highest career Player Efficiency Rating of any player in history, at 27.9

## MICHAEL JORDAN

**18** The 'GOAT' (Greatest Of All Time) according to most people who know their basketball, Michael Jordan still didn't win his first title until his seventh season in the league.

But once he took over, no one else even stood a chance. Topping the league in scoring seven years in a row, leading the Chicago Bulls to three titles on the trot and with history-setting records within reach, he suddenly announced his retirement in 1993 to become a baseball player. However, that segue in his career didn't last long, and only 18 months later he returned to the NBA. Shaking off the rust in the last 17 games of the 1994-95 season, Jordan assumed complete control once again the next season, leading the Bulls to another three straight titles while nabbing another three scoring titles, leaving the question over who the 'GOAT' really is answered once and for all. He promptly retired, again, but returned in 2001 with the Washington Wizards for two more seasons before calling time for good at 39 years old. Jordan won five MVP awards, is fourth on the league's all-time scoring list with 32,292 and third in steals with 2,514. No one has yet bettered his 30.1 points-per-game career average, and no active player seems likely to do so.

LeBron is already considered the greatest player of all time by some basketball experts

## LEBRON JAMES

**19** Only one player today can lay claim to ever upending Michael Jordan in the 'GOAT' debate, and that's LeBron James.

'King James' has been a dominant force since he entered the league in 2003, and is still going strong. LeBron won two titles with the Miami Heat in 2012 and 2013 before returning to his hometown team in Cleveland and leading the Cavs to their first-ever title in 2016. The four-time MVP is now plying his trade for the LA Lakers in search of even more titles, and will surely make a run at Kareem Abdul-Jabbar's all-time scoring record of 38,387 points before he retires. Only Michael Jordan is ahead of LeBron's career PER of 27.7, and he's fourth in combined Win Shares, with plenty left in the tank to rival Kareem's record.

## CHARLES BARKLEY

**20** Charles Barkley defied his critics throughout his career, and despite never winning the title in his 16 seasons in the league, Barkley still made a big mark on the league.

Despite giving up several inches to most opposing power forwards, Barkley averaged 11.7 rebounds per game in his career

At only 6' 6" tall, he was one of the greatest rebounders in the NBA's modern era, and a formidable scorer too. He led the league in rebounds in 1987, at 14.6 per game, and was named the 1993 MVP, making the finals that season. He was (and is) a big character too, divisive on and off the court, but never failing to entertain.

## TIM DUNCAN

**21** While many of the greatest players in history had flashy go-to moves, were high-flying dunkers or had a fiery demeanour, Tim Duncan earned his nickname, 'The Big Fundamental' with his signature understated approach to the game.

His go-to move was a bank shot from the elbow, his celebrations were rarely animated and he approached every game with an almost workmanlike mentality. However, you'd be hard-pressed to find a more competitive player and a more driven winner than Duncan. Playing with the San Antonio Spurs his entire career, Duncan first helped build a dynasty in the Texas city, alongside center David Robinson, and then maintained it himself throughout the 2000s and into the 2010s with his super-consistent, never-back-down style of play. He won five titles with the Spurs from 1999 to 2014, winning two MVP awards, three Finals MVP awards, making the All-NBA first team ten times and the All-Defensive first team eight times. He played 1,392 games in his career, all for the Spurs, finishing his career 14th on the all time list for points (26,496), sixth in rebounds (15,091) and fifth in blocks (3,020). He embodied a philosophy that defined the Spurs team for two decades, one that still endures today after his retirement.

Tim Duncan: not flashy, but a reliable workhorse

# 50 ICONIC NBA PLAYERS

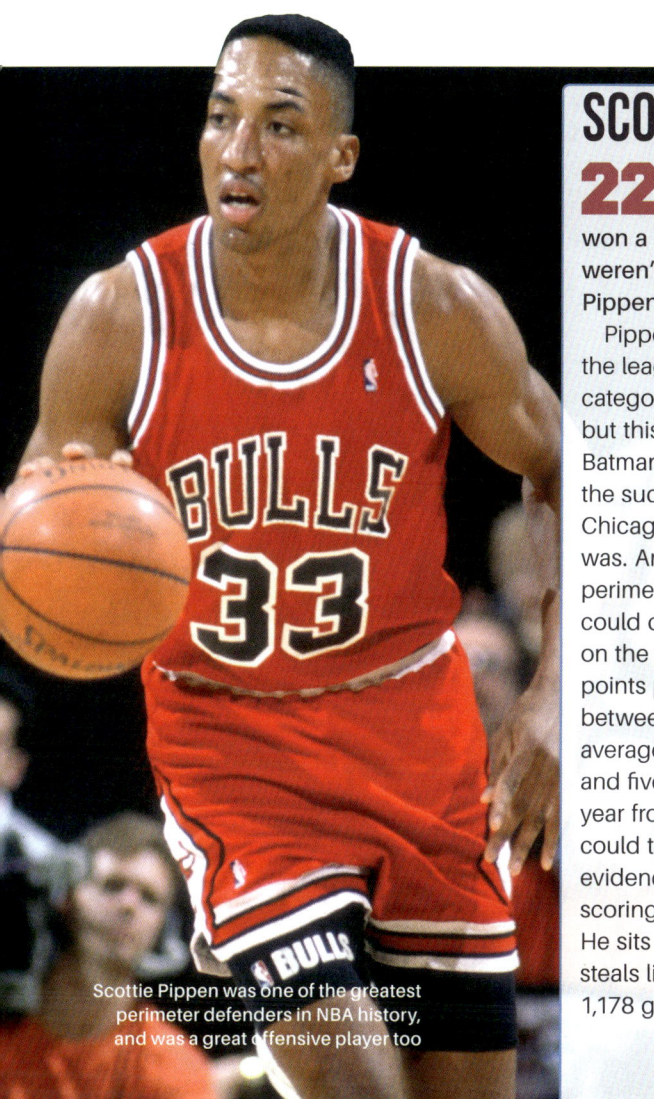

Scottie Pippen was one of the greatest perimeter defenders in NBA history, and was a great offensive player too

## SCOTTIE PIPPEN

**22** Michael Jordan may well never have won a single NBA title if it weren't for Scottie Maurice Pippen.

Pippen only ever led the league in one stat category, steals in 1994-95, but this Robin to Jordan's Batman was as integral to the success of the 1990s' Chicago Bulls as Jordan was. An all-time elite perimeter defender, Pippen could do a bit of everything on the court; he topped 20 points per game four times between 1991 and 1997, he averaged five-plus rebounds and five-plus assists every year from 1989 to 2000, and could take over if needed, as evidenced by his five games scoring 40 points or more. He sits sixth on the career steals list, with 2,307 in his 1,178 games.

## KEVIN DURANT

**23** If you want a masterclass in how to make basketball look simple, just watch Kevin Durant for a few minutes.

The veteran forward holds a career average of 27 points per game, and has perhaps never made a single one of his baskets look difficult. Durant led the league in scoring four times with the Oklahoma City Thunder, but joined the Golden State Warriors in 2016 in his mission for an NBA title, one he finally accomplished in June 2017 and repeated in 2018.

## DAVID ROBINSON

**25** 'The Admiral' won two titles, an MVP award and a scoring title in 1995, and was named Defensive Player of the Year in 1992, but Robinson might still be one of the most underrated players of the whole modern era.

A dominant center, he led the league in rebounds once and blocks once, and laid the groundwork for an enduring dynasty at San Antonio Spurs.

## DWYANE WADE

**24** One of the most electrifying shooting guards of this century so far, and a proven winner.

A three-time champion, and two-time All-NBA First Team selectee, Wade led the league in scoring in 2008-09 at 30.2 points per game.

# NBA LEGENDS

## CLYDE DREXLER

**26** Almost perpetually stuck in the shadow of Michael Jordan, Drexler finally won a title in 1995 after joining the Houston Rockets.

He averaged an impressive 20.4 points, 6.4 rebounds, 5.6 assists and 2.0 steals per game over his career.

## ISIAH THOMAS

**27** Thomas led his Detroit Pistons to two titles in 1989 and 1990, winning the Finals MVP award in 1990.

A proven scorer, he led the league in assists in 1984-85, with an astonishing 13.9 per game and is seventh on the all-time assists list with 9,061.

## JOHN HAVLICEK

**28** Few players have won more titles than John Havlicek, as the Hall of Famer won a staggering eight titles with the Celtics between 1963 and 1976.

He only won one Finals MVP award, in 1974, but the durable Havlicek is recognised today as one of the greatest small forwards in league history.

Larry Bird was one of the two biggest icons of 1980s NBA basketball, along with Magic Johnson

## LARRY BIRD

**29** His career was cut short by injuries, so today Larry Bird doesn't appear on too many all-time leaderboards, but there is one category where he will always reign supreme: pure, unfiltered will to win.

Never the most naturally talented, the extremely hard-working Bird won three MVP awards and was twice named Finals MVP on his way to three titles with the Boston Celtics in the 1980s. Known for his ruthlessly physical style of play, Bird enjoyed getting into his opponents' heads as much as he loved unleashing his unrivalled shooting talent against them. The four-time free-throw percentage leader was the first member of the very select '50-40-90 club' when he shot .525 from the field, .400 from three-point range and .910 from the charity stripe in 1986-87. Despite being plagued with back problems throughout much of his career, Bird holds amazing career averages of 24.3 points, 10.0 rebounds and 6.3 assists per game.

## ALLEN IVERSON

**30** A four-time scoring champion, Iverson was named MVP in 2000-01, and came agonisingly close to winning the title with the 76ers that year. Iverson would never lift the trophy but still secured his Hall of Fame entry through an electrifying career.

Topping 30 points per game four times in his career, 'The Answer' also led the league in steals per game three times, averaging an impressive 26.7ppg and 2.2spg for his career. The shoot-first-ask-questions-later point guard made three All-NBA First Teams and commanded attention throughout his career, even in his final journeyman seasons in Detroit and Memphis, which were riddled with injuries from his time in Philly and Denver, where he led the league in minutes per game seven times.

# 50 ICONIC NBA PLAYERS

Robert Parish had ruthless gameplay

## PATRICK EWING

**31** When highly touted Patrick Ewing joined the league in 1985, many doubted his offensive capabilities, discounting him as a defender with limited offensive upside. How wrong they were.

Ewing went on to top 20 points per game for all of his 13 first seasons, becoming one of the greatest offensive centers in the modern game, while blocking more than two shots per game for 14 straight seasons to boot.

## ROBERT PARISH

**32** Few players embody longevity better than Celtics center Robert Parish. He played 1,611 games over 21 successful seasons, more than anyone else in NBA history.

Although he was a rarely used substitute for his final, title-winning season with the Bulls in 1997, he was an instrumental part of the Celtics that won three rings in the 1980s. Extremely tough on the court, he developed a fierce rivalry with players like the Lakers' Kareem Abdul-Jabbar and perhaps even more famously Bill Laimbeer of the Detroit Pistons. He's the eighth-leading rebounder in NBA history with 14,715 and tenth in blocks, with 2,361.

Stockton only missed four games from 1984 to 1997, and was renowned for his tough play on the court

## JOHN STOCKTON

**33** The NBA's all-time assists leader, and one of the toughest defenders in its history came into the league as a scrawny kid from a small university, but would leave a permanent mark on it, even though he never won the elusive NBA trophy.

Forming a deadly duo with teammate Karl Malone, Stockton led the league in assists an amazing nine times, topping out at 14.5 assists per game in 1989-90, and his reign at the top of the all-time chart with 15,806 won't be challenged for a long time. He's also the league's all-time steals leader with 3,265.

# NBA LEGENDS

## MAGIC JOHNSON

**34** Few players have electrified the NBA like Earvin 'Magic' Johnson did on his arrival to an embattled, financially struggling league in 1979. Incredibly tall for a point guard at 6' 9", Magic had better court vision than just about any player in the league's history, and a creative mind which he put to full use for the 'Showtime' Lakers of the 1980s.

Famously stepping into the center role in the decisive game of the 1980 Finals, he could play any role on the court, which helped the Lakers win an impressive five titles between 1980 and 1988. In 1991, the triple MVP and Finals MVP winner announced his shock retirement as he had been diagnosed with HIV, becoming a leading force in finding a successful treatment to the incurable disease. He returned for 32 games in 1995-96. Now in complete remission from the disease, he's the president of the Los Angeles Lakers.

## RAY ALLEN

**35** Only one player in history has topped Reggie Miller's proclivity from the three-point line, and that man is the ten-time All-Star and two-time champion Ray Allen.

After lighting up the league for a decade with Milwaukee and Seattle, Allen joined Boston in 2007 in order to finally collect a ring of his own, which he duly won in 2008. He repeated the trick in 2013, then a backup player for the Miami Heat. The all-time leader in threes at 2,973 was inducted into the Hall of Fame in 2018, four years after his glittering career, spanning four teams and 1,300 games, came to an end.

It's Miller time: Indiana Pacers alumnus Reggie

## REGGIE MILLER

**36** The Indiana Pacers haven't had as much success in the NBA as they did in the ABA, where they won three titles.

The closest they've come to a title in their 42 years in the NBA came during shooting guard Reggie Miller's prime in the 1990s. Frustrated by the dominance of Eastern Conference rivals, first the Detroit Pistons and then the Bulls for much of the decade, the tenacious competitor and one of the league's first great three-point shooters, finally made it all the way to the Finals in 1999-00. Once there, Miller's heroics pushed the star-studded Lakers to six games before losing to Shaquille O'Neal's monstrous performance. Miller twice led the league in three-pointers made and four times in free throw percentage, and he made five All-Star games. He's still the league's second-leading all-time three-point shooter and has the second-highest Offensive Rating in league history. He averaged 18.2 points per game in his regular-season career, but was famous for stepping up in the playoffs, eight times topping 23 points per game in the postseason, including a team-leading 24.0ppg during the Pacers' lone Finals run in 2000.

## BILL RUSSELL

**37** The defensive yin to Wilt Chamberlain's offensive yang in the late-1950s and through the 1960s, Bill Russell is considered by many to be the greatest ever NBA defender.

He never set the world alight on offense, but he proved better than anyone that you can win with defense: he won an outrageous 11 titles in his 13-year career, all with the Celtics. He led the league in rebounding five times, and if blocks had been counted during his time in the league, the five-time MVP and second-leading all-time rebounder (21,620) would probably be the all-time NBA leader.

## KAREEM ABDUL-JABBAR

**38** Entering the league just as Wilt Chamberlain and Bill Russell's careers were winding down, Lew Alcindor – who converted to Islam and changed his name after winning his first title in 1971 – was the perfect heir to the NBA throne.

An inspiration on and off the court, unstoppable in the NBA and a fierce human rights campaigner outside of it, he realised the influence he could wield as a celebrity and role model and still applies that influence today. On the court, he won six MVPs, two Finals MVPs, won six rings with the Bucks and Lakers, led the league in scoring twice, four times in blocked shots and once in rebounding. He was selected to a record 19 All-Star teams, and is still the league's all-time career scoring leader, with 38,387 points. Only Robert Parish has played more than Jabbar's 1,560 games, and only Russell and Chamberlain tallied more rebounds. He's also third in career blocks, at 3,189 – a fact made even more unbelievable when blocks weren't even counted during his first four seasons.

Kareem Abdul-Jabbar: all-time great and star of *Airplane!*

The high-flying Harden's nickname is 'The Beard' – it's not difficult to see why

## JAMES HARDEN

**39** Few active players can rival Harden's incredible athletic talent and offensive prowess. The double reigning league scoring champion (he scored 36.1 points per game in 2018-19 and 30.4 the season before) can also pass with the best of them; he led the league in assists per game in 2016-17.

After playing as a sixth man with the Oklahoma City Thunder for three seasons, he became a superstar with the Houston Rockets after joining prior to the 2012-13 season. Yet to win an NBA championship, Harden has improved as a defender and become more efficient in recent years, too, so we might not even have seen the best of him yet.

# NBA LEGENDS

Dominique Wilkins in familiar territory – few were as prolific or creative dunkers as Wilkins

## GEORGE GERVIN

**41** Before the San Antonio Spurs' golden era, which has lasted from 1997 to today, Spurs fans had few things to celebrate as part of the NBA.

Among the rare treasures was George 'The Iceman' Gervin, an amazing offensive talent and four-time NBA scoring leader. He followed the Spurs franchise from the ABA to the NBA after the former folded in 1976. From 1976 to 1982, Gervin was almost unstoppable, topping 32 points per game in both 1979-80 and 1981-82, specialising in his signature floating jumper, which was impossible to block. He made the playoffs eight times in nine years with the Spurs, and was selected in five All-NBA First Teams in a row from 1978 to 1982. In the last regular-season game of the 1977-78 season, Gervin famously scored 63 points against the New Orleans Jazz to secure his scoring title – without even playing the fourth quarter! Although he never won a ring, Gervin was rightfully inducted into the Hall of Fame in 1996. Gervin's scoring average of 26.2 in his NBA career ranks ninth all-time.

## DOMINIQUE WILKINS

**40** The French-born Dominique Wilkins was one of the most exciting players in the league from 1982 to 1995, and his many scoring showdowns with archrival Michael Jordan are the stuff of legend today.

Doubtlessly the greatest player to ever wear an Atlanta Hawks jersey, Wilkins was the 1985-86 scoring champion with 30.3 points per game, and would have had two more scoring titles if it weren't for Jordan. He was also a strong rebounder for a small forward, and could hit it from downtown, a skill he gradually honed throughout his career. Fittingly nicknamed 'The Human Highlight Reel', Wilkins regrettably never experienced much postseason success, due to a lack of a strong supporting cast in Atlanta, never making it beyond the Eastern Conference Semifinals. Despite his lack of postseason success, his many in-game and dunk-contest highlights will live forever in NBA legend.

## WALT FRAZIER

**42** The New York Knicks have only won the NBA title twice, in 1970 and 1973.

Without point guard Frazier that tally would probably still stand at zero. One of the league's best two-way players, Frazier made seven All-Defensive First Teams and four All-NBA First Teams, and he was an integral part of the Knicks' two title runs. If he hadn't been hampered by injuries that shortened his Hall of Fame career, the seven-time All-Star's status today would be even more legendary than it is.

## 50 ICONIC NBA PLAYERS    25

At 6' 1" and only 150lbs (185cm and 68kg), Archibald was smaller and lighter than most of his NBA opponents

## RUSSELL WESTBROOK

**44** If anyone thought Oscar Robertson's record of averaging a triple-double for a whole season was unbreakable, Russell Westbrook made it his job to prove them wrong.

Perhaps the most impressive stat-stuffer of the NBA's modern era, Westbrook has averaged a triple-double not once, not twice, but three times in a row in the last three seasons. A competitive point guard, Westbrook has led the league in scoring and assists twice, winning the MVP award in 2016-17. He is still in his prime, so there is little reason to expect he'll give up his history-chasing statistical run anytime soon.

Westbrook averaged 31.6 points, 10.7 rebounds and 10.4 assists per game in 2016-17, winning the MVP award

## TINY ARCHIBALD

**43** Nate 'Tiny' Archibald had an interesting career.

A fantastic scorer in his early career, he broke the record for points per game for a guard (34.0) and total assists (910) in the same season in 1972-73, becoming the only player to lead the NBA in both points and assists per game in the same season. After suffering a bad achilles tendon injury, Archibald sat out a whole season in 1977-78, and returned a much-changed player, now with the Boston Celtics. Gone was the highlight-reel scoring, but instead Archibald became a composed floor general, helping the Celtics to the 1981 NBA title. After eventually hanging up his trainers in 1984, Archibald was inducted into the Hall of Fame in 1991.

# NBA LEGENDS

## RICK BARRY

**45** Rick Barry is perhaps best known as one of the greatest free-throw shooters of all time, famously shooting them underhand – style be damned!

But while he did lead the league in free-throw percentage six times, he was also one of the greatest offensive players of his era. He led the NBA with 35.6 points per game in 1966-67 before joining the ambitious ABA. However, after a few seasons there, Barry was lured back to the NBA, where he led the Warriors to the 1975 title, while scoring 30.2 points per game and leading the league in steals (2.9) to boot. As a mark of his talent, his three sons, Brent, Drew and Jon, all played in the NBA, but all three combined weren't able to match Rick's career total of 18,395 points.

## PAUL PIERCE

**46** In an era of rare drought for the Boston Celtics, Paul Pierce emerged as their new beacon of hope in 1998.

But despite seven straight seasons of 21-plus-point seasons from 2000 to 2007, postseason success still eluded Pierce. With the addition of Kevin Garnett and Ray Allen in the 2007 offseason, Pierce no longer needed to do it all for the Celtics, so despite his scoring numbers dipping, he led the team to its first title in 22 years in 2008. Pierce is the second-leading scorer in Celtics history, topping legends like Larry Bird and Bill Russell.

The sixth man; long-running Celtics bencher McHale

## KEVIN MCHALE

**47** Most of the NBA's most famous icons started most of the games they played throughout their careers, but Kevin McHale, arguably one of the Boston Celtics' greatest players ever, only played four of his 13 seasons for the Celtics as a full-time starter.

The rest of the time, he was quite simply the most devastating sixth man the league has ever seen, only starting due to injuries to other players. Making up a third of the Celtics' 'Big Three' during the 1980s, he formed an ultra-physical, relentlessly competitive and frankly fearsome trio with Larry Bird and Robert Parish, helping Boston win three titles along the way. 6' 10" tall, mobile and ferociously strong, McHale was frequently deployed to defend the opposition's strongest player, often to give them a sneaky elbow in the back as much as defending them legally on the ball. He topped 20 points a game for five seasons in a row from 1985 to 1990, coming sixth in the league in 1986-87 at 26.1, and was a prolific shot-blocker, topping two blocks per game five times. He also led the league in field goal percentage twice and was named to seven All-Star games. Due to his perennial second-fiddle status, he was never named MVP, but won the Sixth Man of the Year award twice, in 1984 and 1985.

## 50 ICONIC NBA PLAYERS

## CARMELO ANTHONY

**48** Considered by some the greatest offensive player of the 21st century, few have ever been as adept at creating their own shot as Denver Nuggets and New York Knicks legend Carmelo Anthony.

He's only led the league in scoring once, but the ten-time All-Star came very close on several occasions. Perhaps more than his already-impressive NBA career, Melo's legacy will endure based on his international career. The only NBA player in history to have won three Olympic golds, his USA career has already assured Melo of a Hall of Fame induction after he eventually retires.

## BOB PETTIT

**49** Two-time MVP Bob Pettit was one of the most dominant players of the NBA in the 1950s and early 1960s.

The powerful center and power forward led the league in scoring twice while playing for the St Louis Hawks, and never dipped below 12.4 rebounds per game. Also an adept passer, he averaged 3.0 assists per game, and he led the Hawks to their first and so far only title, in 1958. The Hawks made the Finals four times during Pettit's tenure with the team before the Celtics assumed complete authority over the league in the 1960s. Pettit is also famous for being the first recipient of the MVP award. He made the All-NBA First Team ten times in his 11-year career. He trails only Bill Russell and Wilt Chamberlain in career rebounds per game with 16.2, and his 26.4ppg rank eighth of all-time.

## GARY PAYTON

**50** One of the most imposing perimeter defenders of the last three decades, Gary Payton built his Hall of Fame career on stingy defensive play, leading the league in steals in 1995-96.

The tough-as-nails Payton didn't miss many games either, only sitting out a combined 15 games in his first 16 seasons. He was very limited offensively in his first few seasons, mainly playing as a facilitator, but would develop into a prolific scorer, and from 1994 to 2003, Payton only failed to eclipse the 20ppg mark twice. Despite all his success with the Seattle SuperSonics, the NBA title always eluded him. In order to chase down that ring, he spent a year playing for the Milwaukee Bucks, then the LA Lakers and after that the Boston Celtics before finally landing the trophy in 2006, then as a backup point guard for the Miami Heat, where he concluded his career a year later.

Payton's nickname was 'The Glove', as he had such supreme talent in stealing and keeping hold of the ball

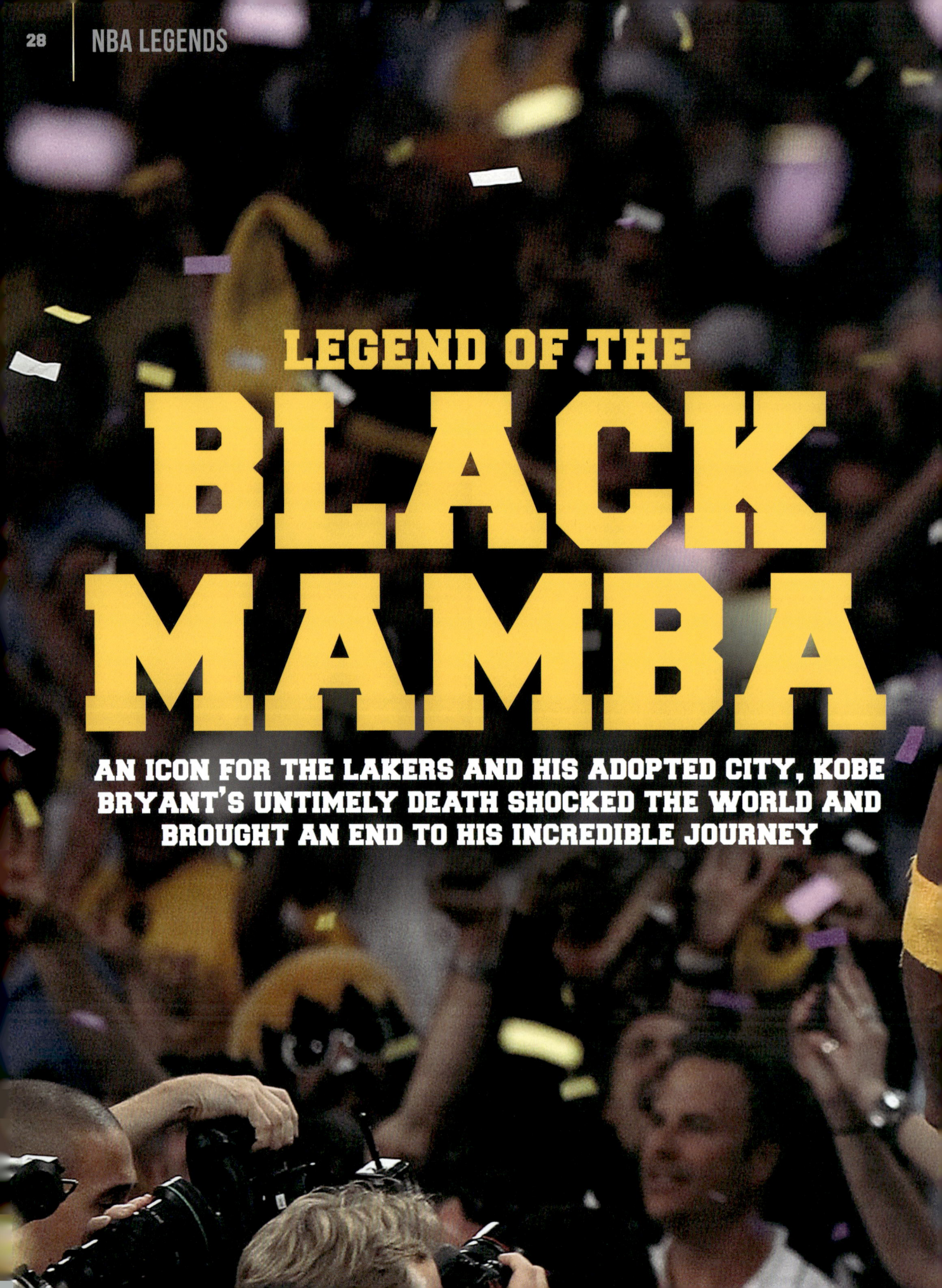

# NBA LEGENDS

## LEGEND OF THE BLACK MAMBA

AN ICON FOR THE LAKERS AND HIS ADOPTED CITY, KOBE BRYANT'S UNTIMELY DEATH SHOCKED THE WORLD AND BROUGHT AN END TO HIS INCREDIBLE JOURNEY

Kobe Bryant enjoyed one of the longest and most decorated careers in NBA history, winning five titles

## KOBE BRYANT

**POSITION:** Shooting Guard
**NBA DRAFT:** 1996/Round 1/Pick 13
**CAREER:** LA Lakers (1996-2016)

• • • •

### HIGHLIGHTS:
5x NBA Champion (2000-02, 2009, 2010)
2x NBA Finals MVP (2009, 2010)
1x NBA MVP (2008)
18x NBA All-Star Team (1998, 2000-16)
15x All-NBA Team (1999-2013)
9x NBA All-Defensive First Team (2000, 2003, 2004, 2006-11)
2x NBA scoring champion (2006, 2007)

### STATS:
#### Regular Season
Points: 33,643 | Assists: 6,306 | Steals: 1,944

#### Playoffs
Points: 5,640 | Assists: 1,040 | Steals: 310

# NBA LEGENDS

Bryant probably bore the greatest responsibility, after Jordan himself, for widening basketball's appeal

"BRYANT WAS DESCRIBED AS ONE OF THE GREATEST PLAYERS OF HIS GENERATION, [BRIDGING] THE ERAS OF MICHAEL JORDAN AND LEBRON JAMES"

Kobe Bryant's sudden and untimely death, in the first month of the new decade, provoked an unprecedented outpouring of grief across the world.

The tragic helicopter crash in southern California – which also claimed the lives of eight others, including his 13-year-old daughter, Gianna – dominated news headlines in every corner of the globe for weeks. There is no doubt that the 41-year-old ex-Laker was a star in Los Angeles and the basketball community. But there are very few sportsmen whose death would have struck such a chord with so many – from Paris to Beijing, Rio de Janeiro to Cairo.

In the weeks following his death, he was described as one of the greatest players of his generation, which provided the bridge between the eras of Michael Jordan and LeBron James.

A transcendent personality, Bryant probably bore the greatest responsibility, after Jordan himself, for widening the sport's appeal beyond North America. So how did this ball player join the ranks of athletes, such as Serena and Tiger, so famous they are known only by a single name?

Kobe had an atypical upbringing for a basketball star. He spent much of his early childhood in Italy after his father, former NBA star Joe 'Jellybean' Bryant, moved the family to play for a series of teams in the European leagues. There, Bryant immersed himself in the local culture – learning Italian and developing a love for football club AC Milan – while also watching NBA games from afar.

Returning to the United States, he lit up varsity basketball at Lower Merion High School in the Philadelphia suburbs, being named a McDonald's All-American and the 1996 Naismith High School Player of the Year in his senior season.

As a teenager, Bryant had already played in scrimmages with the local Philadelphia 76ers, and reportedly made an impression with head coach John Lucas. Nevertheless, it was widely expected he would graduate to one of the country's top basketball colleges – either Duke, Michigan, North Carolina or Villanova.

But unusually and somewhat controversially, Bryant elected to skip college, becoming only the second high-school player to go straight to the NBA in 20 years.

Before the draft, Bryant once again trained with a pro team – this time the Los Angeles Lakers. He ended up being drafted 13th overall by the Charlotte Hornets, in a pre-arranged trade with Los Angeles. That same day, he was sent out west by the Hornets, who later confirmed they had never intended on signing Bryant.

Bryant struggled to adapt to the league, as would be expected of any 18 year old – especially one thrust into the spotlight of one of the league's most important markets. While he impressed his coaches with his work ethic and fierce competitiveness, he initially struggled for minutes, playing an average of little more than 15 minutes a game.

Bryant made some notable strides in his rookie season, winning the 1997 Slam Dunk Contest; claiming the records for the youngest player to play and start in NBA games; and earning a spot on the NBA All-Rookie Second Team.

Perhaps most significantly, he and the larger-than-life center Shaquille O'Neal – also a new arrival in Los Angeles in the summer

During the 2001-2002 season, the Los Angeles Lakers were dogged by reports of the feud between Bryant and O'Neal

# KOBE BRYANT | 31

## KOBE'S 81-POINT GAME

### IN JANUARY 2006, THE LAKERS STAR BURNED THE TORONTO RAPTORS IN A PERFORMANCE BETTERED ONLY ONCE

In 1962, Wilt Chamberlain smashed the single-game scoring record with a mind-blowing 100 points against the New York Knicks. It was widely acknowledged that no one would ever come close to threatening his total.

Until, of course, Kobe Bryant stepped onto the Staples Center court against the Raptors in 2006. He would later tell reporters that he couldn't have envisaged such a perfect night of scoring, hitting 28 of his 46 shots, including seven three-pointers and 18 out of 20 free throws.

"Not even in my dreams," he said. "To sit here and say I grasp what happened, that would be lying."

Bryant finished the second half by scoring 55 points. What set this magical game apart was that his team was in danger of losing it until the last. Los Angeles trailed by 18 in the third quarter, before Bryant went on a tear.

After sealing the game, and smashing Elgin Baylor's previous Lakers record of 71 points in a single game, Bryant left the court to deafening chants of "M-V-P".

Bryant was on fire against the Raptors in January 2006 as he recorded his best-ever scoring performance

of 1996 – began to forge an on-court partnership and an off-court hostility that would go down in basketball folklore.

The season would end on a crushing note, though, when the Lakers were dumped out of the Western Conference Semifinals by Utah by four games to one. Thrust into a crucial role towards the end of the fifth match by injuries and ejections, Bryant shot four air-balls as the Jazz won 98-93 in overtime. O'Neal would later praise Bryant for being "the only guy who had the guts at the time to take shots like that".

He further established himself as one of the sport's best guards over the next two seasons – breaking into the All-Star Team as a starter along the way. But postseason disappointment for the Lakers became an annual feature.

Another elimination at the hands of the Utah Jazz, this time in the Conference Finals, was followed by a crushing defeat by the San Antonio Spurs in the 1999 Western Conference Semifinals. Both were clean sweeps.

The 1999-2000 season was a pivotal one for Bryant and the

# NBA LEGENDS

Kobe is greeted by his wife Vanessa and daughters Natalia and Gianna in 2008

There are few sportsmen whose death would have struck such a chord with so many – from Paris to Beijing and Rio de Janeiro to Cairo

### "Tensions finally came to the boil: Bryant perceived a lack of commitment on O'Neal's part, while Shaq disapproved of Kobe's arrogance"

Lakers organisation. The hiring of legendary coach Phil Jackson sparked a shift in the balance of the team. Jackson, the architect of the six NBA titles won by Jordan's Chicago Bulls in the 1990s, chose not to make Bryant the primary focus of the offense.

Bryant had begun to attract attention for the striking similarity of his game to Jordan's and was identified by many as the heir apparent to His Airness. But ironically, it was O'Neal, the league's best big man, who took the starring role.

The pair's relationship only worsened as LA transformed into a winning machine. The team was perhaps most dominant in the first of the 'three-peat' seasons, finishing the regular season as the best team in basketball. O'Neal won the MVP award as the Lakers went 67-15, completing one of the greatest seasons in the league's history.

The number one-seeded Lakers side duly made their way through the Western Conference – facing particularly stern tests from the Sacramento Kings and Portland Trail Blazers. They then got the better of the Indiana Pacers in six games in the Finals.

Bryant was playing second fiddle to O'Neal. He came up with a clutch 25-point performance with 11 rebounds and four blocks in Game 7 of the Western Conference Finals against Portland. He also hit the winning shot in Game 6 of the Finals, clinching the championship.

O'Neal was the star of the show, though. He would be awarded the first of his three NBA Finals MVP awards. By the time they reached the following year's playoffs, the Lakers were considered one of the best teams ever.

After Bryant recorded an improved statistical year in 2000–2001 – averaging 28.5 points per game – the Lakers swept through the post-season. They took the title with the loss of just one game against Allen Iverson's Philadelphia 76ers in the Finals, having swept each of their three opponents in the Western Conference bracket. The team's 15-1 postseason record is second only to the Golden State Warriors' 16-1 playoff run in 2017.

Bryant's game took a giant stride forward the following year. He played all but two games in the 2001–2002 season and recorded a then personal high of 56 points in a game against the Memphis Grizzlies. He also won his first All-Star Game's MVP crown.

His Lakers team, once again, comfortably made the postseason with a 58-24 record but, in the West, it was the upstart Sacramento Kings who took the top seed into the playoffs. After sweeping the Trail Blazers in the first round, Los Angeles easily dispensed with the San Antonio Spurs and league MVP Tim Duncan.

But it was the 2002 Western Conference Finals against the Kings – whom the Lakers had vanquished in the previous two seasons – that would go down in infamy. To this day, it is still considered one of the most exciting series in NBA history, as well as the most contentious.

Bryant was a perennial All-Star and was one of the elite shooting guards in the game

*The 2002 Western Conference Finals against the Sacramento Kings were infamous, thanks in part to Bryant's elbow to Mike Bibby's face*

Los Angeles were dogged by reports of the worsening feud between Bryant and O'Neal. Headlines during the 2001-2002 season were often dominated by reports of O'Neal's inadequate fitness levels – allegedly a major source of Bryant's dissatisfaction.

While many expected the reigning champions to step up the intensity and breeze through, the Kings were not so obliging, racing to a 3-2 lead in the series. Game 6 has gone down as one of the most controversial in NBA playoff history. A host of blown refereeing calls in the final minutes favoured the Lakers.

Perhaps the most egregious of all missed calls was Bryant's infamous elbow to Mike Bibby's face, thrown right under the nose of one of the referees. Bibby then missed a three-pointer to tie the game, giving the Lakers the 106-102, with O'Neal top-scoring with 41.

It was followed by a tense Game 7, which saw the lead change 19 times over the course of the match. Bibby, again at the centre of the action after being fouled, made both free throws right at the death, forcing overtime. The Kings' poor shooting handed Los Angeles victory in the end, by a score line of 112-106, in which O'Neal and Bryant scored 35 and 30 points respectively. The NBA Finals were a blowout, with the Lakers sweeping the New Jersey Nets 4-0.

By this time, Bryant was a perennial All-Star, having cemented his reputation as one of the elite shooting guards in the game.

They became only the fifth team in history to win three back-to-back championships (including the 1959-1966 Boston Celtics, who won eight on the bounce). For all the great teams to have come since – including LeBron James's Miami Heat and Steph Curry's Golden State Warriors – the 2000-2002 Lakers are still the last team to three-peat.

The 23-year-old Bryant was the youngest-ever player to win three titles, averaging an impressive 26.8 points per game in the championship series. Once again, though, he was forced to play a supporting role, as O'Neal shone, completing his hat-trick of Finals MVP awards.

## KOBE FINALLY LANDS THE MVP

**BRYANT COULD HAVE NETTED FIVE MVP AWARDS BUT LOST OUT TO STEVE NASH, TIM DUNCAN AND DIRK NOWITZKI**

Not many players win the MVP award – so to suggest Kobe Bryant could feel aggrieved to have only won one may sound churlish. But there were a number of seasons when he had serious claims to be the best player in the world that were ignored.

In 2002-2003, the Lakers guard posted an average of 30 points per game as his team finished 50-32 as defending champs. The award went instead to the San Antonio Spurs' Tim Duncan, who averaged just 23.3 points a game.

Two seasons later, he played another superlative season – although he only appeared in 66 regular seasons games. Bryant watched as Steve Nash picked up the player of the year award. Nash again won the MVP award in 2005-2006, despite Bryant leading the league with 35.4 points a game, 5.3 rebounds and 4.5 assists.

And in 2006-2007 the Dallas Mavericks' Dirk Nowitzki took home the MVP prize, despite Bryant dragging a poor Lakers team to a winning record.

So when Bryant was finally handed the Maurice Podoloff Trophy, for leading LA to the best record in the West in 2007-2008, it felt richly deserved.

*Kobe Bryant defends the Golden State Warriors' Baron Davis in 2007-2008, his only MVP season*

# NBA LEGENDS

**MAMBA MENTALITY**
For all his abilities, what set Kobe Bryant apart was his insatiable desire to always improve – which came to be known as the 'Mamba mentality'.

**KOBE'S TRADEMARK FADEAWAY**
Bryant's deadly fadeaway shot became a familiar sight at the Staples Center, combining his leaping ability with a deft touch for shooting.

**BRYANT PLAYS WITH GRUESOME INJURY**
Despite tearing a ligament in his right pinkie, Bryant elected to defer surgery to play the rest of the season in his 2007-2008 MVP year.

**CAN'T KEEP MAMBA OUT**
Despite tearing his Achilles tendon at the end of the 2012-2013 season, Bryant's famed competitiveness saw him return to the court after just eight months.

**FOOTWORK HONED BY SOCCER**
Bryant was always one of the nimblest and most precise movers in the NBA, largely thanks to a youth spent playing football in Italy.

# KOBE BRYANT

Bryant represented Team USA on a number of occasions, playing in the 2008 and 2012 Olympics in Beijing and London

It was to be the zenith for the partnership. Tensions which had been simmering for years finally came to the boil. Bryant resented his secondary role within the team and perceived a lack of commitment on O'Neal's part, while Shaq disapproved of Kobe's arrogance.

Two disappointing, fractious seasons followed. In a regular season in which he didn't miss a game, Bryant averaged 30 points and went on a run of nine games scoring at least 40 points. The team, though, came up short in the playoffs, as they were eliminated by the San Antonio Spurs in the Conference Semifinals.

Then, in the 2003 offseason, Bryant's world came crashing down. In July, he was arrested and charged by police after a 19-year-old hotel employee accused him of sexual assault at the Lodge and Spa at Cordillera in Edwards, Colorado.

He denied the claims, although he did admit to having an adulterous sexual encounter with the young woman. The case never reached a criminal trial; the charges were dismissed when the complainant informed the court she was unwilling to testify. In March 2005, a civil lawsuit between Bryant and his accuser was settled out of court.

He would spend the remainder of his career and his life attempting to forge a public image based on his role as an elder statesman of the game, as well as a husband and father. Nonetheless, the shadow of the allegations has cast a shadow on his legacy.

It certainly hung over the Lakers' 2003–2004 season. In anticipation of another serious crack at the NBA title, the franchise acquired future Hall of Famers Karl Malone and Gary Payton. After earning another playoff appearance, Los Angeles brushed aside the Houston Rockets, defending champions San Antonio Spurs and the Minnesota Timberwolves to make it to their fourth Finals appearance in five years.

Despite being heavy favourites, it was not to be. Bryant and O'Neal played together for the final time in a 4-1 series upset at the hands of the Detroit Pistons. Upon the departure of O'Neal and the dismissal of coach Phil Jackson, the Lakers then missed the playoffs for the first time in more than a decade.

The 2005–2006 season would prove to be pivotal in Bryant's career. Phil Jackson, the legendary coach who had already accumulated nine rings, came back to Los Angeles, despite previously enduring a turbulent relationship with Bryant.

Almost a year to the day after he was sacked, Jackson returned to the Lakers – reportedly at the urging of Bryant himself. It would lead to a historic revival and Bryant enjoyed a markedly improved statistical season. The team returned to the playoffs but were eliminated in an agonising series with the Phoenix Suns, despite holding a 3-1 lead. It would prove a painful loss.

Starting in the 2006–2007 season, he switched his jersey number from 8 to 24. What followed was a rebirth for Kobe Bryant. It acted as a clear symbol for the start of the second half of his career. As he said himself, he entered the league with a "plant your flag" mentality and "non-stop energy and aggressiveness". But in the wake of the sexual assault allegations, his public feuds and being outshone by O'Neal's Miami Heat, Bryant was at his lowest ebb. The rest of his career would be focused on "growth" and a greater maturity – on and off the court.

The 2007–2008 season was perhaps the finest individual year of his career, and he was awarded his first and only league MVP award. Despite suffering a ligament tear in the little finger on his shooting hand, he played in every regular season game. Alongside new signing Pau Gasol, the Lakers went 57-25 but lost the NBA Finals to the Boston Celtics.

In the next two years, Bryant brought two more championships back to Los Angeles. Bryant starred in the Finals of both and was awarded two series MVP awards. The first triumph came against the Orlando Magic, who were bested by 4-1. In the second, the Lakers got their revenge on the Celtics, overturning a 13-point deficit late on in Game 7. Although the team ultimately missed out on another three-peat, Bryant had finally silenced the critics who argued he couldn't win without O'Neal. Assuming the starring role he had always coveted, Bryant finally delivered.

The last six years of his career brought no further rings, as the cast surrounding Bryant gradually worsened. Los Angeles failed to make the postseason in each of his last three years. Midway through the 2015–2016 season, acknowledging the cumulative effect injuries had had on his body, Bryant called time on his playing career.

Despite being plagued by injuries, he signed off his career in true Kobe style – with a 60-point game against the Jazz. Recognising his status as one of the game's all-time greats, typically hostile crowds in Philadelphia, Sacramento and even Boston honoured him with farewell ovations. Once universally loathed as an enfant terrible, Bryant was now loved for his superhuman drive for perfection.

This would crystallise into his 'Black Mamba' persona, characterised by an unparalleled competitive spirit and an unrelenting will to win.

In his adopted city, he was elevated to the level of an icon. Even in Los Angeles – which welcomed Kareem Abdul-Jabbar, Magic Johnson, Jerry West and Shaquille O'Neal – no athlete has greater embodied the Lakers or the city itself better than he did.

While his complicated legacy will continue to be debated, few players have ever been so devoted to the game of basketball. He will be remembered forever.

## NBA LEGENDS

# AN ICONIC FIGURE

### JERRY WEST IS ONE OF THE NBA'S MOST ICONIC STARS, BUT HE HAD TO ENDURE MORE THAN A DECADE OF HURT BEFORE BECOMING A CHAMPION

West would likely have won more championships if not for the Celtics' dominance

Legends are often valued by the trophies they've won and records they've set during their career. Championship rings, MVP awards, top points scorers – the list goes on. However, sometimes a legend will be more than just their stats and trophy cabinet. They will represent something mere data can't quantify, and one such legend is the iconic LA Lakers stalwart Jerry West.

West only won a single NBA championship title and NBA Finals MVP in his career, but that tally is far from the full story. He reached the Finals nine times and was named in the NBA All-Star team in each of his 14 seasons. He nearly went down in history as the greatest player never to win an NBA championship, but earned a fairytale win in 1972 at the age of 34.

West was one of the NBA's hardest-working players, primarily as a result of his difficult childhood. He was not a natural sportsman, but hours of relentless practice with a hoop outside his neighbour's house in West Virginia made him a ruthless sharpshooter. It was here that he developed his signature moves – the fast release snap-shot that never gave defenders time to close him down. West's appetite for hard work was aided by a sudden growth spurt that took him above six feet. He starred for his high-school team, leading them to the 1956 state title, before taking West Virginia University to the 1959 NCAA finals, losing by a single point to the University of California. Despite the loss, West earned the Most Outstanding Player award, setting the tone for a career in which he gained individual accolades without team success. One team honour he did achieve was 1960 Olympic gold.

West's exploits made him the overall number two draft in 1960 – just behind Oscar Robertson. West headed to LA to join the Lakers, who themselves had just moved from Minneapolis.

West's debut season saw him score 1,389 points and make the NBA All-Star team, but the Lakers lost at the Division Finals stage. They got a step further in 1962, reaching the NBA Finals, where they'd play the Boston Celtics. The Lakers were 3-2 up with two games to play, but fell to an agonising overtime defeat in the deciding game. Four more Finals defeats to the Celtics followed, but, in 1969, despite yet another loss to their great rivals, West

### JERRY WEST
**POSITION:** Point Guard, Shooting Guard
**NBA DRAFT:** 1960/Round 1/Pick 2
**CAREER:** LA Lakers (1960-74)

**HIGHLIGHTS:**
1x NBA Champion (1972)
1x NBA Finals MVP (1969)
14x NBA All-Star Team (1961-74)
1x All-Star MVP (1972)
12x All-NBA Team (1962-73)
4x All-Defensive First Team (1970-73)
1x NBA assists leader (1972)

**STATS:**
**REGULAR SEASON**
Points: 25,192 | Assists: 6,238 | Rebounds: 5,376

**PLAYOFFS**
Points: 4,457 | Assists: 970 | Rebounds: 855

# JERRY WEST

## SIMPLY THE WEST

### WEST'S LEGACY AS A NEARLY-MAN OF BASKETBALL WAS TURNED ON ITS HEAD IN A SUPERB CAREER OFF THE COURT

After retiring as a player in 1974, West returned to the Lakers as head coach two years later. He may not have won a title, but he did return the Lakers to the play-offs after two years without any post-season action.

He was inducted into the Hall of Fame in 1980 before being appointed Lakers' general manager in 1982. The Lakers reached seven Finals in the 12 years West was in charge, winning three. He built one of the greatest teams in NBA history – the 1986-87 title-winning side, featuring the likes of Kareem Abdul-Jabbar, Magic Johnson and James Worthy. He continued his upwards trajectory in his second career, becoming executive vice-president of basketball operations, winning the first of two Executive of the Year awards in 1995. Finally, in 2000, his 40-year association with the Lakers was finally over, although he was immortalised in a statue outside the Staples Center in 2011. However, West's love affair with basketball continued. A stint with the Memphis Grizzlies resulted in a first-ever post-season appearance for the franchise and another Executive of the Year award. He left soon after, but his golden touch continued when he joined the Golden State Warriors in 2011 and oversaw three of their five consecutive NBA Finals appearances. But LA proved too strong a lure, and he returned to head up the Clippers, so expect success there soon.

No one was getting close to West when he was taking one of his blink-and-you-miss-it jump shots

was named the first-ever Finals MVP, the only man to win this while on the losing side.

West's reputation as one of the game's greatest players was immortalised that year when the NBA commissioned a new logo. Alan Siegel wanted an iconic image, and found one in West. A silhouette was created, a logo made and a legend born. Despite the honour, West has said he's not a fan of being the man behind the mask; the famously private star preferring to avoid attention.

It seemed the tide may be turning for West, as he scored a career-high 31.2 points per game in 1969-70, but the playoffs delivered more pain. The Celtics collapsed, leaving only the New York Knicks between West and a first title. The stars seemed to be aligning when West launched a 60-foot buzzer-beater to tie Game 3, but the Lakers again fell to a 4-3 Finals defeat.

But then, in 1972 West finally had his moment. Once again the Lakers faced the Knicks, and a fired-up duo of West and Wilt Chamberlain shot the Lakers to a 4-1 win, the Lakers' first title since 1954. West was finally an NBA champion.

West played two more seasons before finally bowing out, aged 36. He had amassed over 25,000 points, becoming only the third man to reach that mark, as well as an unbroken streak of 14 years as an All-Star.

West may not have the silverware to back up his legend, but most players to follow him will acknowledge that they live in his shadow – quite literally, as that iconic NBA logo shows he truly is an all-time NBA great.

West had a great partnership with Elgin Baylor (left), who retired the year before that incredible 1972 championship win

38 | NBA LEGENDS

Bird scores against the Lakers during the 1987 NBA Finals

# I AM LEGEND

## FOR 13 SEASONS, LARRY BIRD WAS THE BEATING HEART OF THE BOSTON CELTICS, AND MAY JUST HAVE BEEN THE GREATEST PLAYER EVER

When Larry Bird made the decision to retire after 13 seasons as a Boston Celtic, then-NBA commissioner David Stern had no doubts about the impact he had made on the game.

"Quite simply, Larry Bird has helped to define the way a generation of basketball fans has come to view and appreciate the NBA," he said. "In the future, great players will be judged against the standards he has set, but there will never be another Larry Bird."

It was a fitting accolade for a player who helped breathe life into what many considered to be a dying league. Bird's blue-collar work ethic brought new fans into the game, and his rivalry with Magic Johnson of the LA Lakers became the greatest in professional sports. Bird did not save the Boston Celtics – they had a rich heritage, and were in no need of a saviour – but he may have saved the NBA.

Basketball is technically a non-contact sport, but the battering Bird took in his 13 pro seasons, as well as in college and high school before that, left him in no doubt that it was time to get out.

"The pounding and the pain made my decision for me," he said after announcing his retirement in August 1992. "I gave my heart, my body, my soul to the Celtics. For the past 17 years I have put my body through living hell."

Bird was an unlikely superhero. Tall and skinny, he lacked the athleticism of the flashier players when he entered the league in 1979. It was widely touted that he was too slow to make the transition from the college game, and that the bigger, faster men of the professional ranks would be too much for him to handle.

Ultimately, Bird turned in one of the great careers in basketball history, using court awareness, anticipation and basketball IQ to make up for his athletic deficiencies. Technically a small forward, he actually combined elements of many different players. He could match a power forward for size, a guard for grace and touch and a center as a rebounder. He was a hugely talented distributor of the ball, finding teammates with pinpoint passes that could unlock a defense.

He was no shrinking violet, taunting opponents, getting under their skin and sometimes laughing in their faces at their inability to stop him. He was not always popular with his opponents, but he would become defined by his relationship with Magic Johnson – starting out as bitter enemies, they became firm

Bird takes on legendary 76er Julius Erving

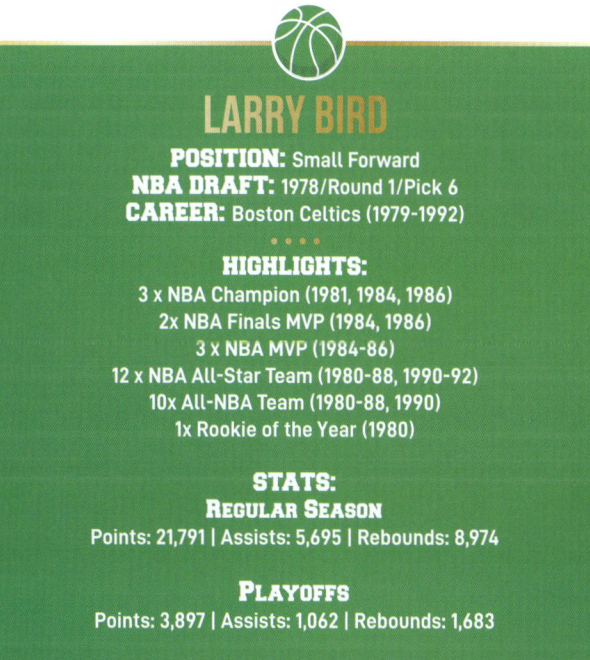

## LARRY BIRD

**POSITION:** Small Forward
**NBA DRAFT:** 1978/Round 1/Pick 6
**CAREER:** Boston Celtics (1979-1992)

### HIGHLIGHTS:
3 x NBA Champion (1981, 1984, 1986)
2x NBA Finals MVP (1984, 1986)
3 x NBA MVP (1984-86)
12 x NBA All-Star Team (1980-88, 1990-92)
10x All-NBA Team (1980-88, 1990)
1x Rookie of the Year (1980)

### STATS:
**REGULAR SEASON**
Points: 21,791 | Assists: 5,695 | Rebounds: 8,974

**PLAYOFFS**
Points: 3,897 | Assists: 1,062 | Rebounds: 1,683

# NBA LEGENDS

The physical Detroit Pistons roughed Bird up during the 1987 Conference Finals

Boston's 'Big Three' - Larry Bird (second left), Kevin McHale (second right) and Robert Parish (right) - wait for their chance on the bench

friends when they actually got to know each other.

Bird's journey started in archetypal small-town USA. Born in West Baden Springs, Indiana, on 7 December 1956, he starred at Springs Valley High School after his family moved to tiny French Lick.

The lanky star was heavily recruited when it came time to move up to the college ranks, but a month at the Indiana University under legendary coach Bobby Knight was enough to convince him that the place was just too big for him. He returned to French Lick (population circa 2,000) to reconsider, before enrolling at the much smaller Indiana State University a year later. Bird transformed the fortunes of the Sycamores, a school that had never made the NCAA tournament in its history.

Bird took them to the postseason for three straight years, culminating in an appearance in the NCAA Final in 1979 with a record of 33-0. In the final, Bird's Sycamores came up against the Spartans of Michigan State, led by one Earvin 'Magic' Johnson. Johnson and the Spartans prevailed, and a legendary rivalry was born.

Foregoing his senior season at Indiana State, Bird joined the Celtics (he was selected with the sixth pick of the 1978 draft, but opted to stay in college for one more season) and made an immediate impact in the pros. The Celtics had 13 NBA titles to their name when Bird joined, the last as recently as 1976, but the team was in a mini slump. Bird helped lift them back into contention, averaging 21.3 points per game as a rookie.

The Celtics improved their number of wins on the previous year by a staggering 32.

Bird's impact was little short of incredible. As a rookie he led the team in points, rebounds and steals. He made the Eastern Conference All-Star squad and had games with 36 and 45 points. He was named the Rookie of the Year. It was an extraordinary arrival for Bird, who was still something of a gangly boy.

"He looked like a little old country bumpkin," recalled long-time Celtics coach and president Red Auerbach. "But when you looked into his eyes you knew you weren't talking to any dummy. He knew what he wanted in life and he knew what it would take to get there."

It was the start of a special era in the Celtics' history. The 1980 draft saw the addition of Kevin McHale (a first-round pick), while Robert Parish joined via a trade. Together with Bird, they would become Boston's 'Big Three', although there was never any doubt over who was the biggest.

Bird was never afraid of hard work. He once commented that he had played well over a thousand games as a Celtic, but reckoned he had played more than that as a kid in his back yard, honing the skills that would serve him so well in the pros.

"On the court, Larry was the only player in the league that I feared and he was the smartest player I ever played against," said archrival Johnson. "I always enjoyed competing against him because he brought out the best in me. Even when we weren't going head to head, I would follow his game because I always

# LARRY BIRD

## THE BEST OF ENEMIES

**The Johnson-Bird rivalry was once the most compelling story in professional sport and helped define an era**

Magic Johnson and Larry Bird became icons to their respective fan bases. More than that, they were cultural symbols at a time when racial tension was running high in the USA.

Both entered the league in 1979. Both enjoyed stunning success in the NBA, and they retired within a year of each other. Johnson helped the Lakers win the league title in his rookie year, and Bird did the same in his second campaign.

With the rivalry dating back to their college days, there was no love lost between the two men.

"He hated me," Johnson claimed in 1987. "I hated him. We really didn't know each other. We didn't even speak. We might hit hands before a game, that's about it."

Bird disagreed, saying, "Hate is a strong word, but I sure wanted to beat him," and in any case, the relationship between the two men underwent a stunning transformation. Working together on a Converse commercial in 1986, they became the best of friends.

"I don't really think of him as a brother," Bird would later say, "but every time I've seen him, I'm always happier. If I ever had an idol, he's probably my idol because he plays the game like I try to play it."

> "BIRD ONCE COMMENTED THAT HE HAD PLAYED WELL OVER A THOUSAND GAMES AS A CELTIC, BUT RECKONED HE HAD PLAYED MORE AS A KID IN HIS BACK YARD"

used his play as a measuring stick against mine."

It was hard to measure up to Bird. In fact, for a period in the mid-1980s, nobody was able to. For three consecutive seasons, from 1984 to 1986, Bird was the league MVP. After his stunning rookie campaign he turned in almost identical numbers in the 1980–81 season, leading the Celtics to their 14th championship.

One play in the first game of the 1981 Finals epitomised Bird's mastery of the sport. Unleashing a shot, he instantly realised it was going to miss, and moved to collect the rebound, which he duly sank. Never the quickest man on the court physically, he made up for this by thinking faster than anyone else.

The triumph kicked off a new era of success for the Celtics, but their mastery of the league was nowhere near as absolute as during the 1950s and 1960s, when they had once made ten NBA Finals in a row. The 1980s Celtics dynasty had to fight for its place at the top of the pile with Johnson's Lakers in a rivalry that came to define the NBA and attract people to the league in

*Bird and Johnson battle it out during their college days*

# NBA LEGENDS

> "Bird helped the Celtics to their third title in six years during the 1985-86 season, winning the league's MVP award"

Bird gets the better of arch rival Magic Johnson in the 1987 NBA Finals

Bird puts pen to paper to sign with the Celtics

their thousands.

The Celtics made five appearances in the NBA Finals in the 1980s, winning three. The Lakers made eight appearances, winning five. The pendulum swung repeatedly as the two behemoths of the sport battled for supremacy in one of the most enthralling and extended rivalries in any sport. It reached a crescendo in 1984.

The Lakers were staking their claim for dominance, having already made the finals three times in the early years of the decade. Their fourth appearance coincided with Bird's second. The Lakers could cement their place at the top of the pecking order, but Bird led his Celtics to the crown in the seventh game. The crescendo lasted, as the franchises traded championships – for years it seemed like no other team was playing.

At the same time, Bird was already beginning to break down under the pressure. In the 1985 Finals, against the Lakers once more, he was slowed by niggling injuries and Los Angeles gained their revenge. In the offseason following that campaign, Bird injured his back clearing his mother's driveway. Blue collar through and through, it was a fitting way for him to pick up an injury, but it would mark the start of an inexorable decline.

Despite the injury, Bird helped the Celtics to their third title in six years in the 1985–86 season. Winning the league's MVP award for the third consecutive year, he was entrenched as the biggest name in the sport.

Bird, however, was not a one-man wrecking ball. He always had solid support from the other components of the Big Three, as well as the rest of the Celtics squad. The difference between a great team and a great player was exemplified in the first round of the 1986 playoffs when Michael Jordan, despite prodigious individual efforts, was unable to overcome the Celtics single-handedly.

In the Finals that year against Houston, Bird was other-worldly. A triple-double (registering double figures in points, rebounds and assists) is the mark of a truly exceptional game. Bird almost averaged a triple-double over the entire six games of the Finals. He averaged 24 points, 9.7 rebounds and 9.5 assists per game.

After reaching such heights, the only way was down. Bird slogged his way through the playoffs the following season, but was battered and bruised by the physical defenses of the Milwaukee Bucks and the Detroit Pistons, emerging as the sport's bad boys. By the time the Celtics limped into the Finals, once more facing Johnson's Lakers, Bird was a spent force and the Lakers won in six games. It was the last time Bird would reach the Finals, while the Bulls and Pistons would take turns to dominate the Eastern Conference and the Lakers would remain competitive in the West.

Bird was far from finished, and enjoyed one of his most statistically impressive seasons in the 1987–88 campaign. Adapting his game to take account of his declining physical skills, he was more apt to shoot from three-point range rather than move inside, where the big men of opposing defenses could dish out punishment. Bird's exceptional shooting skills made this tactic pay off with a 29.9 points-per-game average, the highest of his career. He appeared in 76 out of 82 regular season games, but the passing of the torch was demonstrated when he finished second to Jordan in the league MVP voting.

The following year, Bird's body finally gave out. Appearing in just six games, he then underwent surgery to remove bone spurs in both heels. The Celtics went 42-40.

As a new decade opened, Boston's Big Three were fading out together. Bird was 34 during the 1990–91 season, increasingly slowed and limited by injuries, the most serious of which were his lingering back problems. He was still capable of great performances, registering 45 and 43-point games, but he also missed 22 contests. More surgery followed in the offseason, this time on his back, and he missed 37 games in his next and final season.

On 15 March 1992, in a fine swansong, Bird elevated himself out of a slump to hit 16 points in the final quarter to force overtime against Portland in a game the Celtics eventually won. A stunning 49 points, 14 rebounds and 12 assists made this incredible performance the 59th and final triple-double of his career.

The 1992 Olympics were a comparatively undemanding climax to Bird's playing days. As part of the Dream Team, he won a gold medal in his last game of competitive basketball.

Larry Bird epitomised grit, determination and hard work. His physical skills were not as obvious as the superstars who played against him, but he gave the working man a hero to root for in a league of flashy superstars. His nickname, 'Larry Legend', speaks volumes, but so do the people who were privileged to witness his greatness.

In Red Auerbach's words: "Nobody has ever been more self-motivated. Nobody in my 42 years played hurt the way this guy did. He did it for his love of the game and his love of the people."

## A NEW CHALLENGE

**AFTER DOMINATING ON COURT FOR MOST OF HIS CAREER, BIRD PROVED EQUALLY EFFECTIVE OFF IT AFTER HANGING UP HIS SNEAKERS**

Following retirement as a player, Bird spent five years as a special assistant in the Celtics' front office, but his primary focus was recovering from the brutal experience of 13 years of professional basketball. He played golf and relaxed on the beach for much of the time before he was ready for his next challenge.

That would come back in his home state. Despite having no coaching experience, Bird was named head coach of the Indiana Pacers in 1997. Pledging to hold the job for just three years, Bird made an instant impression, much as he had during his playing days. The Pacers made the Conference Finals in his first two seasons and went all the way to the Finals in his third and last season, losing to (who else?) the Lakers, in six games. Named NBA Coach of the Year in 1998, he returned to the Pacers in 2003 as President of Basketball Operations.

Helping rebuild the franchise, Bird was named the NBA's Executive of the Year for the strike-shortened 2011–12 season. He remains the only man to be named league MVP, Coach of the Year and Executive of the Year.

Having further underlined his place in NBA history, Bird finally retired for good.

Bird during his successful stint as head coach of the Indiana Pacers

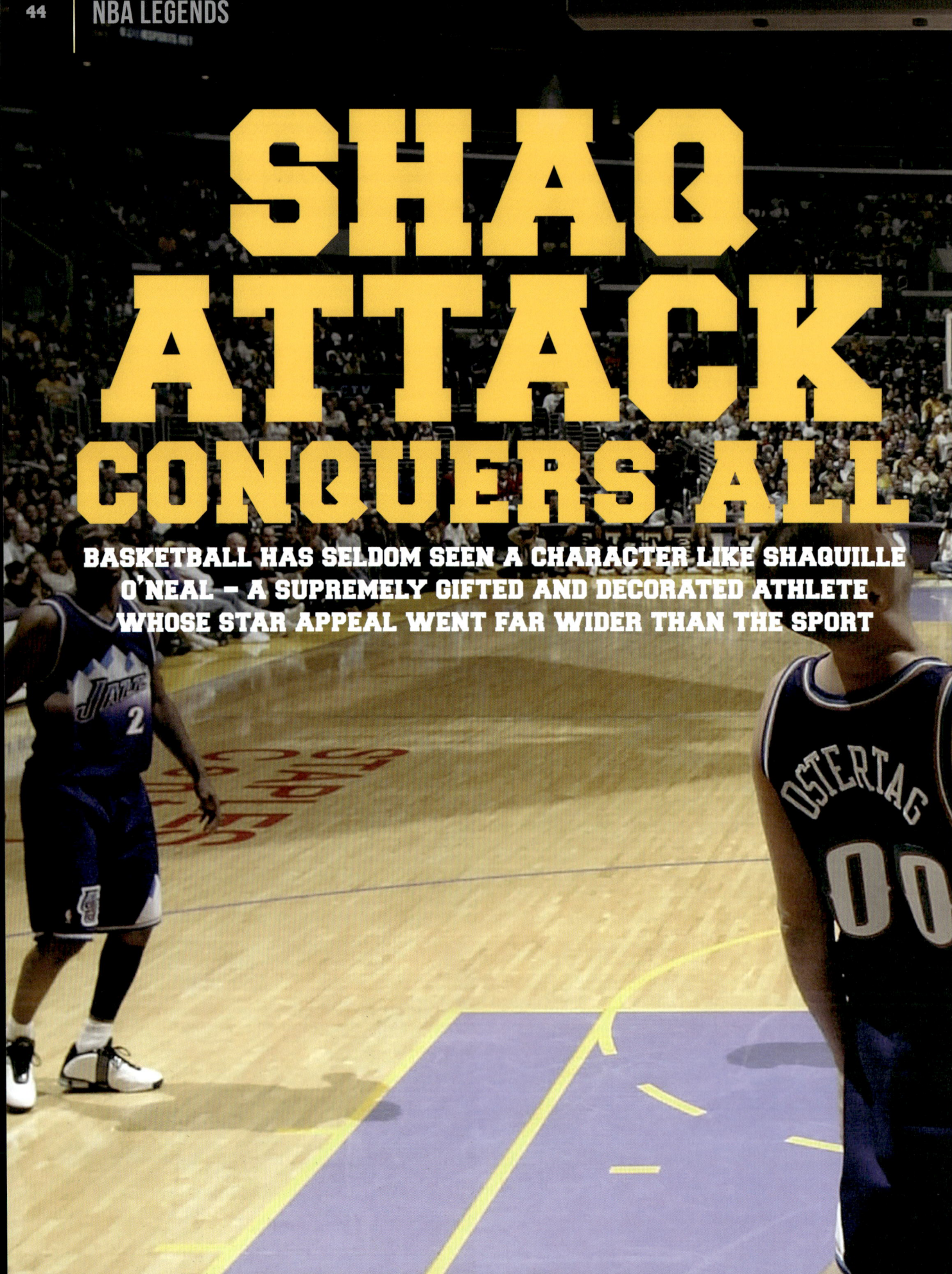

# SHAQ ATTACK
## CONQUERS ALL

BASKETBALL HAS SELDOM SEEN A CHARACTER LIKE SHAQUILLE O'NEAL – A SUPREMELY GIFTED AND DECORATED ATHLETE WHOSE STAR APPEAL WENT FAR WIDER THAN THE SPORT

# SHAQUILLE O'NEAL 45

Greg Ostertag of the Utah Jazz can only look on as Shaq slams home for the Lakers in 2003

## SHAQUILLE O'NEAL
**POSITION:** Center
**NBA DRAFT:** 1992/Round 1/Pick 1
**CAREER:** Orlando Magic (1992-1996), LA Lakers (1996-2004), Miami Heat (2004-2008), Phoenix Suns (2008-2009), Cleveland Cavaliers (2009-2010), Boston Celtics (2010-2011)

### HIGHLIGHTS:
4x NBA Champion (2000-02, 2006)
3x NBA Finals MVP (2000-2002)
1x NBA MVP (2000)
15x NBA All-Star Team (1993-1998, 2000-2007, 2009)
14x All-NBA Team (1994-2006, 2009)
1x Rookie of the Year (1993)
2x NBA scoring champion (1995, 2000)

### STATS:
**Regular Season**
Points: 28,596 | Blocks: 2,732 | Rebounds: 13,099

**Playoffs**
Points: 5,250 | Blocks: 459 | Rebounds: 2,508

# NBA LEGENDS

Shaquille O'Neal holds aloft the MVP trophy and the Larry O'Brien Trophy in June 2000 after beating the Indiana Pacers

O'Neal had a lucrative career off the basketball court, releasing a number of hip-hop records during his career

Shaquille O'Neal is enormous in every way. Standing at 7-feet 1-inch and weighing 325lbs, the four-time NBA champion was one of the most physically dominant basketball players who ever lived. His sheer physical gifts were not the only reason for his success, as is sometimes suggested – but his overwhelming physicality was impossible to ignore.

But he also boasted one of the biggest personalities the game has ever seen. In many ways, he set the template for modern sportsmen as builders of personal 'brands' off the court.

He acted in movies, recorded four albums and has starred in countless television programmes. The man known simply by the mononym 'Shaq', was also a favourite of basketball beat writers looking for a snappy quote.

Upon his retirement, in 2011, many of those same journalists said the lasting impression they had of O'Neal was of a fun-loving showman. This was in sharp contrast to the public image of his one-time teammate and nemesis, Kobe Bryant, who was all business, on and off the court.

ESPN's Michael Wilbon wrote that it was the "fun and games" he associated most with Shaq, while Mark Heisler of the Los Angeles Times described O'Neal as "the giant who kept the NBA laughing", adding that he "gave us 19 years of tons of fun".

His shooting from the free-throw line was comically bad at times. With averages from the foul line hovering around 75 per cent, Shaq's career percentage of 52.7 per cent did little to dispel his image as something of a joker. But for all that bluster and outward charisma, it is quite easy sometimes to forget how large a shadow he cast over the rest of the NBA in his prime.

For a time, after the retirement of Michael Jordan and before the peaks of Kobe Bryant and LeBron James, Shaq was both the best and the most important basketball player in the world. He was the central piece in the Los Angeles Lakers team that won three consecutive NBA championships, winning Finals MVP awards in each of the years and taking the league MVP prize in the 1999-2000 season.

His prime years may not have lasted all that long. But if an NBA star is judged on the peaks he reaches – rather than his longevity – then O'Neal has a strong claim to be one of the best centers to have played the game. Perhaps, even, he was the second greatest ever, behind Kareem Abdul-Jabbar. Shaq's claim to greatness is boosted by the fact that he was the most dominant center at a time when big men reigned supreme.

Over his career, which spanned between 1992 and 2011, O'Neal faced off against Yao Ming, Patrick Ewing, Hakeem Olajuwon, Dikembe Mutombo and David Robinson – and was better than all of them. He was also deceptively skilled for a ball player of his size. At his physical peak, he was known to hit jump shots and spin moves. But it was his sheer size and power which set Shaq apart from all others. The league even had to design new backboards after he pulled two down on slam dunks during his 1992-93 rookie season.

Born in 1972 in Newark, New Jersey, O'Neal spent part of his childhood in San Antonio, Texas, near to where his army sergeant stepfather was based. It was there he began to attract national

# SHAQUILLE O'NEAL

Shaquille O'Neal makes a slam dunk in a playoff game against the Sacramento Kings in 2001

**"The man known simply by the mononym 'Shaq', was also a favourite of basketball beat writers looking for a snappy quote"**

## THE PEAK OF SHAQ'S POWER
### THE GREATEST PERFORMANCE OF O'NEAL'S NBA CAREER UNDERLINED HIS LEGEND

Shaquille O'Neal delivered one of the most dominant displays in recent sporting history on 6 March 2000 – his 28th birthday.

The irrepressible center finished the game with a career-high 61 points on 24-for-35 shooting, 23 rebounds and three assists in the 123-103 win over the LA Clippers. True to form, his free-throw shooting let him down, making just 13 of 22 attempts.

Shaq was in irresistible form that night and playing at the very height of his powers in the dismantling of the Lakers' crosstown rivals.

Reflecting on the game, he explained: "A couple of my teammates said they wanted me to get 50, so I just tried to get the ball in a deep position, and they looked for me. I have to thank my teammates and coach Jackson for giving me an opportunity to do that."

At one stage of the game, O'Neal hit 15 straight points – rounded off with a dunk off a feed from Kobe Bryant. He exited the game with three minutes left.

The historic game against the Clippers would prove to be a sign of things to come; months later Shaq would be voted a near-unanimous MVP and the Lakers would win the first of three consecutive NBA championships.

Shaq scores a layup on his way to a career-high 61 points against the LA Clippers on 6 March 2000

attention, both for his remarkable height and prodigious skill on the basketball court.

After leading Robert G Cole High School to a 68-1 record in two years, which also saw him claim a state championship in his senior year, O'Neal won a place at Louisiana State University.

Shaq continued his remarkable upward trajectory at college, where he was a two-time All-American. In his time with the LSU Tigers, he was also named the best college basketball player in the country by the NCAA in 1991 – as well as by the Associated Press. Today, a bronze statue of O'Neal stands in front of LSU's basketball practice facility. That earned him the number one spot in the 1992 NBA draft, where he was chosen by the Orlando Magic above future Hall of Famer Alonzo Mourning, as well as All-Stars Christian Laettner and Tom Gugliotta.

He made an instant impact, becoming the first player to win the Player of the Week award in his first week in the league. Averaging 23.4 points a game on an astonishing 56.2 per cent shooting and 13.9 rebounds per game, O'Neal took home the Rookie of the Year award. On the way, he helped the Magic improve their record by 20 games in just one season.

He went from strength to strength the following year, pushing his points per game average up to 29.4. Paired with rookie Penny Hardaway, Shaq got Orlando up to a remarkable 50 wins. It was the first time that the franchise, founded in 1989, had made the playoffs where they were eliminated in the first round by the Indiana Pacers. He led the league in scoring in his third year, finishing second in MVP voting. Heading back to the playoffs with a 57-25 record, O'Neal took the team all the way to the 1995 NBA Finals. The fairytale run saw the Magic beat the Boston Celtics by three games to one, before eliminating the Chicago Bulls and the Pacers in six and seven games respectively.

It was not to be a dream ending for O'Neal, however. Series MVP Hakeem Olajuwon had an inspired series and, paired with fellow future Hall of Famer Clyde Drexler, led the Houston Rockets to a 4-0 sweep of Orlando.

Shaq would play just one more season in Orlando – and spent much of it out injured. Nevertheless, he would average more than 26 points per game as the Magic finished second in the Eastern Conference in a 60-22 regular season. But their season was once again ended in a 4-0 series loss, this time by Michael Jordan's irrepressible Chicago Bulls in the Conference Finals. It would be

# NBA LEGENDS

## A CAREER OF PARTNERSHIPS

**OVER THE COURSE OF HIS ILLUSTRIOUS NBA CAREER, O'NEAL FORMED FORMIDABLE PARTNERSHIPS**

For all of his on-court brilliance, Shaq was never the easiest guy to play alongside.

Much has been made of his legendary falling out with Kobe Bryant, which brought one of the most successful partnerships in sports history to a juddering halt. Both joined the Lakers in 1996, later forming the axis of the side that achieved a historic three-peat between 2000 and 2002.

Eventually, tensions that had simmered for years reached boiling point in the 2004 offseason, when O'Neal was traded to the Heat. Some mourned the senseless feud – including NBA coach Doc Rivers, who reportedly called it the "biggest travesty in sports".

In Miami he struck up a close relationship with youngster Dwyane Wade. Under Shaq's guidance, Wade would mature into an elite shooting guard. In their second season together, the pair won an NBA title as Wade took centre stage, winning a Finals MVP award. He would later indicate that Shaq had a bigger impact on his career than any other teammate. Later O'Neal teamed up with Steve Nash – with whom he endured a frosty relationship – before uniting with LeBron James.

Shaq, pictured here with Steve Nash while playing for the Phoenix Suns, did not always enjoy good relationships with teammates

Shaq spent a year playing with LeBron James at the Cavaliers before retiring

> "SHAQ WILL BE BEST REMEMBERED FOR HIS LARGER-THAN-LIFE CHARACTER. HIS STYLE OF PLAY MAY HAVE BEEN UTTERLY DOMINANT, YET UNMISTAKABLY JOYOUS"

the last time he would wear the Magic's uniform. Now a free agent, Shaq could hear Hollywood calling his name. He packed his bags and headed West, teaming up with the Lakers. Shortly after Team USA arrived in Atlanta for the 1996 Olympic Games, it was reported in the press that O'Neal would be signing a seven-year contract with the Lakers. After taking gold with Dream Team III, he made an immediate impact in Los Angeles in his first two seasons. Although he missed 31 games in the 1996-97 season, he scored 26.2 points a game and helped the team win 56 games.

He quickly endeared himself to the Lakers fans, and was unafraid of unleashing a fierce competitive spirit on the court. In his first playoff game for the franchise, against the Portland Trail Blazers, he scored a whopping 46 points. But despite his explosive start, the Lakers were dumped out by the Utah Jazz, who would go on to reach the NBA Finals.

Utah would be their vanquishers the following season, too. The disappointment felt by Lakers fans is hard to overstate. With four players on the roster – Shaq, Kobe Bryant, Nick Van Exel and Eddie Jones – making the All-Star Team, the sense was that the Los Angeles team were on the cusp of something special. But the legendary Jazz pairing of Karl Malone and John Stockton were too good, sweeping the Lakers 4-0 in the Western Conference Finals.

And Kobe and Shaq made it a trio of missed opportunities in the next campaign, which was shortened by a lockout. It was a year of flux, with a number of the Lakers' established stars being moved on in search of a winning formula. After struggling to a 31-19 record, the team was knocked out in the Conference Semifinals by San Antonio, the eventual champions. But if Shaq's first three seasons in Los Angeles each ended in disappointment, the next three would go down in NBA history.

Phil Jackson, the celebrated coach behind the Chicago Bulls' two 'three-peats', rolled into town and brought the triangle offense with him, kicking off a new basketball dynasty. Under the tutelage of Jackson, O'Neal also made leaps on the defensive side of his game, maturing into an all-round threat.

The 1999-2000 season may have been the finest of the center's legendary career. He won the NBA scoring title and was just one vote shy of becoming the league's first-ever unanimous choice for MVP. It was also one of the greatest seasons in the franchise's history. The team won 31 of their first 36 games and finished with a 67-15 – the club's highest win total since the 1986-87 season, when they won their tenth NBA title. Discovering a newfound steel, Los Angeles squeaked past the Sacramento Kings and the Portland Trail Blazers – in the first round and Conference Finals respectively – before overpowering Reggie Miller's Indiana Pacers in six games in the NBA

# SHAQUILLE O'NEAL

Finals. The following year was the mirror-image – the Lakers won 11 fewer games but breezed through the playoffs.

Sweeping the Portland Trail Blazers, Sacramento Kings and the San Antonio Spurs to reach the NBA Finals, Los Angeles defeated MVP Allen Iverson and the Philadelphia 76ers 4-1 to win their second consecutive title.

The historic treble was completed the following year. After beating the spirited Sacramento Kings in the Western Conference Finals in one of the greatest playoff series of all time, the Lakers swept the New Jersey Nets in the NBA Finals. O'Neal was named as the series MVP in all three winning NBA Finals, playing the central role in one of the most dominant NBA sides in history. For Shaq, his place in history was sealed – even though cracks were beginning to appear in the off-court relationship between he and Kobe Bryant.

Bryant, desperate to be the face of the Lakers franchise, was frustrated by playing in the supporting role to Shaq – while O'Neal was rubbed up the wrong way by Kobe's abrasive, lone-wolf persona. Dreams of a four-peat were extinguished with a playoff loss to San Antonio which ended their 2002-03 season, while an allegation of sexual assault against Bryant cast a dark cloud over the 2003-2004 campaign.

The Lakers did manage to reach the NBA Finals in 2004 – their fourth in five years – but would lose to the Detroit Pistons, spelling the end for the Kobe-Shaq era.

Whether Shaq's trade to the Miami Heat was motivated by the Lakers' preference to retain Kobe Bryant or their refusal to grant O'Neal a pay rise is a matter of conjecture.

Either way, he found himself back in Florida, contending for supremacy in the Eastern Conference alongside the up-and-coming Dwyane Wade.

Shaq was revived, playing more games in a season than he had since 2000-01. In his first season on the team, the Heat surged to the best regular season record in the Eastern Conference, and he narrowly missed out on the MVP award to Steve Nash. After defeat in the 2005 Eastern Conference Finals, the Heat would claim its first ever NBA crown the following season.

Shaq delivered one of the performances of his career against a youthful Chicago Bulls team in the first round of the playoffs, scoring 27 points and delivering 16 rebounds in Game 1. He then drained 28 points to seal the Conference Finals against the Pistons in six games.

Miami completed its championship season by taking down the much-fancied Dallas Mavericks in the title-decider – winning four games on the spin after dropping the first two games of the series.

Shaq would chase a fifth ring for the rest of his career – staying in Miami until 2008, before spending a season each with the Phoenix Suns, Cleveland Cavaliers and Boston Celtics.

As the injuries gradually became more frequent, O'Neal called it quits after the 2010-11 season. Aside from his four rings and three NBA Finals MVP awards, he also boasts 15 All-Star selections in 19 seasons of professional basketball. But more than the awards and trophies, Shaq will be best remembered for his larger-than-life character. His style of play may have been utterly dominant, yet unmistakably joyous.

The souring of the relationship between Shaq and Kobe is the stuff of NBA legend

Image source: Getty Images

## NBA LEGENDS

# 10 OF THE NBA'S GREATEST COACHES

**Although not as visible as the great teams and players, the NBA's finest coaches have shaped the game from the sidelines**

In the 70-plus year history of the league, more than 300 men have held the coveted job of head coach in the NBA. Each of them performed in their own way, but most failed to truly make their mark. Many different criteria go into a successful career. Winning titles, building dominant teams and simply surviving in a cut-throat world can all mark a coach out from the crowd. A select few have managed to combine all of these into truly exceptional careers, but some men coached for decades despite never winning a championship, while others had short careers that were crowned with multiple titles.

These ten men found different ways to succeed in a sport where failure is not tolerated for long. Some harnessed great players, some built great teams and some brought innovative ways of playing to the court. Some became synonymous with a single franchise, and others had success at multiple stops along the way. They coached for 11 seasons, 20 seasons or 32 seasons, but all left their mark on the game, and none of them will ever be forgotten.

Jackson's ability to manage superstar talents like Michael Jordan was his defining feature

## PHIL JACKSON
### THE ZEN MASTER

**01** When conversation turns to the greatest NBA coach of all time, it is difficult to look past Phil Jackson. His winning percentage of 70.4 is unrivalled and allowed him to rack up 1,155 regular season wins in 20 years as a coach.

The addition of 229 playoff victories (at a 68.8 winning percentage) is impressive enough before you factor in the 11 NBA championships. Jackson, apparently, was uncertain of how to lose, and although some point to the stellar players he had at his disposal, with both the Bulls and the Lakers, it is impossible to write off his success as pure luck.

Jackson's taste for NBA titles might have developed as a player, where he won two over a 12-year career. That is more than respectable, but as a coach he operated on a different level. In an era where player power was growing, along with player egos, Jackson was able to keep his teams functioning smoothly.

Yes, he had talents like Michael Jordan and Scottie Pippen in Chicago, and Shaquille O'Neal and Kobe Bryant in LA, but handling superstars is a task in itself. Jackson employed unconventional methods, reading Eastern philosophy and earning the nickname of 'the Zen Master'. His approach may have been unconventional, but the results were spectacular. Six NBA titles in seven seasons is an amazing accomplishment, but Jackson not only accomplished that from 1996 to 2002, he did it while coaching two teams, splitting the titles equally between the Bulls and the Lakers.

On the court, Jackson was a disciple of the triangle offense, and had one of the system's key innovators, Tex Winter, on his staff with both the Bulls and the Lakers. The offense is cited as key in the development of Jordan, who had been targeted by opposing defenses prior to its installation in 1989. The following season, the Bulls won their first NBA title on their way to six championships in eight years.

Jackson's philosophy is neatly encapsulated in the many quotes attributed to him, including the one that sums up his beliefs around the sport best of all: "Good teams become great ones when the members trust each other enough to surrender the Me for the We."

He also had a sense of humour. "If you meet the Buddha in the lane," he said, "feed him the ball."

# NBA LEGENDS

Wilkens in 1994 as coach of the Atlanta Hawks

## LENNY WILKENS
### STAYING POWER

**02** Some consider the length of Lenny Wilkens' career as somehow undermining his achievements, but anybody who cracks the thousand-win barrier is going to be in the conversation when talk turns to great coaches.

Wilkens coached for an incredible 32 seasons, and although he only landed a single NBA title, his 1,332 regular season wins are only bettered by Don Nelson, with the still-active Gregg Popovich closing in. Coach of the Year with the Atlanta Hawks in 1994, he won a gold medal as coach at the Atlanta Olympics two years later.

Wilkens coached in Seattle, Portland, Cleveland, Atlanta, Toronto and New York, and as if that wasn't enough of a challenge, he was a player-coach for his first four seasons. Wilkens was no slouch as a player either, making nine All-Star appearances. He is in the NBA Hall of Fame as both a player and a coach, and is also in the College Hall of Fame as a player.

## LARRY BROWN
### THE RESTLESS SOUL

**03** Brown coached for 26 seasons in the NBA, following four in the American Basketball Association, but he refused to settle down. Denver, New Jersey, San Antonio, LA (Clippers), Indiana, Philadelphia, Detroit, New York and Charlotte were all stops on his NBA journey.

His six-year spell in Philadelphia was the nearest he came to putting down roots, and his restlessness earned him the distinction of being the only man to coach two NBA teams during the same season, leading San Antonio for the first half of the 1991–92 season, and the LA Clippers for the second.

His most successful period was a two-year stint with the Pistons, in which he took his team to consecutive NBA Finals (winning the first and losing the second). He guided eight of his nine NBA teams to the post-season, with only the 2005–06 Knicks missing out.

More than a thousand regular season wins proved he knew what he was doing. He also won a college championship (with the Jayhawks of Kansas University in 1988), and is the only coach to pull off that double.

Brown celebrates with his Detroit Pistons after winning the 2004 NBA Finals

# 10 OF THE NBA'S GREATEST COACHES

Kundla is held aloft by his players after one of their many wins

Images source: Getty Images/Sporting_News

## PAT RILEY
### MR SHOWTIME

**05** Pat Riley is almost as famous for his style as he is for his coaching achievements. Suave and immaculately turned out, he looked more like a fashion designer than a coach, but that was only part of his story. Along with the sharp suits and slicked-back hair, he won basketball games at a frightening rate.

A career winning percentage of 63.6 is impressive, but he was hitting well above that during stints with the Lakers and Knicks, before some tough years in Miami brought his average down. He won four titles with the Lakers between 1982 and 1988, and was rewarded for sticking with the struggling Heat for 12 seasons by landing his fifth championship in 2006.

Riley was able to excel wherever he went, winning Coach of the Year awards at all three of his coaching destinations, but he will be best remembered for his time with the Lakers, where he ushered in the 'Showtime' era with superstars Kareem Abdul-Jabbar and Magic Johnson.

The LA roots ran deep – Riley also won a championship with the Lakers as a player in 1972, and his legend is only enhanced by the fact that he is one of few men bold enough to guarantee a championship win. Joe Namath did it for the New York Jets in the week before Super Bowl III, but Riley outdid even Namath, guaranteeing the Lakers would repeat immediately after their 1987 championship. Naturally, the Lakers fulfilled on his promise.

## JOHN KUNDLA
### THE LAKERS LEGEND

**04** John Kundla had one the shortest careers of any of the men on this list – just 11 seasons – and his 423 regular season wins is a positively modest amount. But the 60 playoff wins he added included five NBA championships in a six-year span, from 1949 to 1954. Four sub-par seasons at the end of his career brought his winning percentage down to 58.3, but his Minneapolis Lakers squad missed the playoffs just once under his leadership.

The Lakers (originally named in honour of Minnesota's status as the 'Land of 10,000 Lakes') were the NBA's first dynasty, and Kundla had multiple Hall of Famers in his squad. The match almost never happened though, as Kundla initially turned down the chance to jump to the pro game until an eye-watering $6,000 per season was offered.

Minneapolis, of course, would relocate to Los Angeles and enjoy tremendous success there as well.

Riley, pictured with Magic Johnson, won four championships with the Lakers

# NBA LEGENDS

Popovich talks tactics with Tim Duncan during a game against the Minnesota Timberwolves in 1999

## GREGG POPOVICH
### THE INSIDE HIRE

**06** There are many ways to land a job as an NBA head coach. Gregg Popovich took an unusual route, hiring himself in his capacity as general manager of the San Antonio Spurs. It was a bold move (he had no NBA head coaching experience at the time), but it paid off quickly.

From sixth in the old Midwest Division in his first season (1996–97), the Spurs climbed to second in his second campaign and were NBA champions at the end of his third. Four further titles followed, and in the 2015–16 season the Spurs racked up a gaudy winning percentage of 81.7. He has been named Coach of the Year three times, in 2003, 2012 and 2014.

Still at the helm in San Antonio, at the age of 71, Popovich is also the current coach of the US national team and is expected to lead them at the Tokyo Olympics. At the time of writing he has 1,269 regular season wins over 24 seasons with the Spurs, an NBA record for a coach with a single team. If playoff games are included, no coach in NBA history has more wins than Popovich – and he's still going.

## CHUCK DALY
### THE MOTOWN MAESTRO

**07** Chuck Daly was fired from his first job as an NBA head coach after winning just nine of 41 games with Cleveland in the 1981-82 season. He had no reason to be ashamed – he was the third man to try coaching the Cavaliers that season, and he bounced back in a big way with the Detroit Pistons, starting in 1983.

The Pistons were the NBA's bad boys, and Daly helped ensure their confrontational ways did not go too far, leading them to nine straight playoff berths and three NBA Finals, from 1988 to 1990. The Pistons' two titles, in 1989 and 1990, came with a combined 8-1 record as they bullied the Lakers and Trail Blazers respectively.

As with so many of the NBA's greats, both players and coaches, Daly had his taste of Olympic glory in 1992, coaching the Dream Team to a gold medal. He then rounded out his career with two seasons as coach of New Jersey and two with Orlando, whom he led to a Division title in his final season as a coach.

*Chuck Daly, pictured with Isiah Thomas, during his stint with the Detroit Pistons*

# NBA LEGENDS

## DON NELSON
### THE NEARLY MAN

**08** Nelson was an innovator and a coach who proved you don't need the biggest names in the game to have success. The NBA championship might have eluded him, but he still racked up 1,335 regular season wins – more than any other coach in NBA history.

What mars Nelson's record (and almost kept him out of this list) is his paltry 75 playoff victories. By contrast, Phil Jackson had 229 playoff wins, and he coached for just 20 seasons.

Nevertheless, over 31 campaigns as a head coach, Nelson landed eight Division titles, with his best performances coming in Milwaukee. Three times the Bucks lost in the Conference Finals, and Nelson had a last shot at the big game in 2003, when Dallas also bowed out at the Conference Finals stage. The 'point forward' concept was his, as was the intentional fouling tactic known as 'Hack-a-Shaq', developed when he was with the Mavericks, giving Nelson a legacy beyond his win-loss record.

Nelson coaching the Milwaukee Bucks in 1983

## JERRY SLOAN
### ALL THAT JAZZ

**09** Some coaches hop around, but Jerry Sloan knew he was home when he took over as head coach at Utah in 1988. Following four seasons as an assistant coach with the Jazz, Sloan was comfortable with these surroundings and saw no reason to leave for more than 22 seasons. He finally resigned, having never brought a title to the Jazz and citing a loss of energy, during the 2010-11 season, but over 1,000 regular season wins is enough to earn a place in the pantheon of great coaches.

Sloan was a hard task master, and led his team to 15 straight playoff appearances, including Western Conference titles in 1997 and 1998 (in both Finals he lost to his old team from his playing days, the Chicago Bulls). Sloan's tenure coincided with the reign of Karl Malone as the big name in the Jazz line-up, and the two men worked together for 18 seasons.

As a player, Sloan is revered as the 'Original Bull' for his exploits with Chicago. His number four Bulls jersey has been retired.

Sloan with his Utah Jazz team in 1999 during a game with the Houston Rockets

# RED AUERBACH
## THE SERIAL WINNER

**10** Auerbach amassed nine NBA titles, just two fewer than Phil Jackson, despite coaching for three fewer seasons. As with Jackson, some people attribute the deluge of titles to the talented players Auerbach worked with, most notably Bill Russell.

There may be mileage in the notion, and it is true that Russell landed two more titles with the Celtics after Auerbach retired following the 1965–66 season, but the coach must be credited for building his team around a defensive giant when offensive statistics ruled the roost.

Orchestrating a trade for Russell after the 1956 NBA draft would have been enough to enshrine Auerbach in Celtics lore (Russell became the fulcrum of the Celtics, and is regarded as possibly the greatest defensive player in league history), but he did much more than that. Teamwork and defensive stoutness were Auerbach's watchwords, and he is credited as a key innovator in the 'fast break' offense, which stressed moving the ball quickly once in possession, before the opposing defense had time to organise properly.

In a troubled era for American race relations, Auerbach was a pioneer. He was the first coach to draft an African-American player (Charles 'Chuck' Cooper, in 1950) and he also sent an all-African-American starting line-up onto the court in 1964. The winner of the NBA Coach of the Year award now receives the Red Auerbach Trophy, and his 938 career wins (including three seasons in the Basketball Association of America) was a record when he retired from coaching in 1966. No fewer than 30 of the players Auerbach coached went on to have their own coaching careers, while 14 of his charges are now enshrined in the NBA Hall of Fame, as is Auerbach himself.

After moving into the Celtics front office, Auerbach helped bring another seven NBA titles to Boston, but he was not always the most popular character in basketball. The competitive fires that burned inside him could sometimes rage out of control, and he was infamous for occasionally lighting up a victory cigar during home fixtures – while the game was still going on.

Auerbach's final foray in coaching came in 1984, when he took the reins of a veterans team at the All-Star Game. Age had not dimmed his competitive spirit, and he was ejected for arguing with the officials.

Auerbach with the legendary Bill Russell, on their way to nine titles in ten seasons

## NBA LEGENDS

# 23 REASONS JORDAN IS THE GREATEST

### FROM HIS INCREDIBLE DEBUT SEASON TO LAUNCHING THE MOST ICONIC BRAND IN SPORT, THIS IS WHY MICHAEL JORDAN IS BASKETBALL

Open a dictionary on either side of the Atlantic, look up the word 'basketball' and you won't find a single word of definition – all you'll see is a picture of Michael Jordan soaring through the air, tongue hanging out, awestruck opponents gazing up at him.

This is what MJ means to the sport of basketball. He's a living legend. A man who took one of America's greatest professional sports and made it a global phenomenon. Forget the Harlem Globetrotters, Jordan became a true mainstream icon thanks to his incredible footwork, deft ball handling and heart-stopping dunks. Put simply, Michael Jordan is to basketball what the late, great Muhammad Ali was to boxing – a definitive two-word synonym for the sport.

As testament to this, we've gathered together 23 moments that encapsulate MJ's dominance of the NBA, along with five potential challengers to his throne. Records broken, championships claimed, and legendary status achieved: this is the momentous history of basketball's most iconic son.

# 23 REASONS JORDAN IS THE GREATEST

## CLINCHING RING NUMBER SIX WITH THE CHICAGO BULLS

**01** Some might argue that Jordan – and the Bulls' – first NBA title in 1991 was the greatest moment of his career, but truth be told the original championship clinch was the inevitable end to a six-year build up that cemented Jordan's status as a superstar.

But a sixth title in the same decade? Now that's the stuff of sporting legend.

That final game, a rematch against the Utah Jazz on 14 June 1998 was a close one. The Jazz gave no Bulls no quarter, and with 40 seconds left on the clock and the Bulls trailing, Jordan would again prove his greatness. Two expert shots later, the second from a Jordan steal, saw the Bulls clinch the title at the buzzer. Six titles, one decade. Jordan's final shot for the Bulls was a magical moment in time.

## 'THE SHOT'

**02** In the late 1980s, Jordan was fast becoming the face of basketball thanks to his speed, point-scoring power and instant likeability.

And as the Bulls entered game five of the Eastern Conference first-round series on 7 May 1989 he would perform a single move that would echo through the history of the NBA. Facing the third-seeded Cleveland Cavaliers, who the Bulls had struggled against in the regular season, a tight match-up looked to be heading back to Chicago for game six. But Jordan and company weren't going down without a fight. As the game drew to a close with the Cavs in the lead, Jordan took a shot from the foul line and hit a buzzer-beating basket that would send the Bulls through.

# NBA LEGENDS

## THE FLU GAME

**03** Imagine playing one of the best games of your career while battling a nasty case of the flu and a 103-degree fever. It sounds paradoxical, if not outright impossible.

Well, as history proves, Jordan was no ordinary player, and healthy or not, he was not going to sit on the sidelines and abandon the Bulls when they needed him the most. Dubbed 'The Flu Game', the match-up between Chicago and the Utah Jazz in game five of the 1998 NBA finals saw Jordan step up and score an incredible 38 points while fatigued and disoriented. Coach Phil Jackson unequivocally called it the best Jordan performance he's ever seen, and this was MJ on a bad day. Two days later, he and the Bulls claimed their fifth title.

## THE HALL OF FAME

**04** It's not often that a Hall of Fame speech makes its way into the annals of sporting history.

On 11 September 2009, Michael Jordan was finally inducted into the hallowed halls of the NBA HOF and when he stepped up to the mic he made waves by bringing up every single person who had doubted him, from his earliest years to his arrival in the NBA. He didn't attack them, however. Instead, he thanked them, citing them as a driving force for his success. Controversially, Jordan even called out former GM Jerry Krause, who had gone on record stating only organisations could win championships. Jordan was defiant in his position – it was players, not franchises, that won titles.

## A FATHER'S DAY NBA TITLE

**05** When Michael Jordan's father was murdered in 1993, he swiftly announced his retirement from basketball, citing a lack of enthusiasm for the sport now that his biggest fan had been taken from him.

His Airness would go on to have a middling career in Major League Baseball before returning to the NBA, and the Bulls, in 1995. He was immediately able to rekindle the fire that had made him so dominant in the years before. Jordan would go on to help the Bulls win another NBA title, the fourth of his career, with the championship-winning game coming on Father's Day: a true tribute to the late James Jordan.

## A PLAYOFFS RECORD OF 63 POINTS

**06** During the 1986 NBA Playoffs, Michael Jordan would secure another record. In a match-up against the Boston Celtics on 20 April 1986, he scored a truly terrifying 63 points and helped secure a powerful Bulls victory.

It's a towering record, and one that still stands, continuing to cement Jordan's status as one of the NBA's most creative and dominant players. On that day, Jordan was unstoppable – he'd been out for most of the regular season with a broken foot, but when he returned he ravaged the Celtics. It was such an incredible performance that Celtics legend Bird commented that he'd come up against "God disguised as Michael Jordan."

## 23 REASONS JORDAN IS THE GREATEST

## SHRUGGING OFF GREATNESS

**07** If there was one event that could sum up the palpable sense of magic surrounding Michael Jordan in his heyday, it's 'The Shrug'.

One of several epochal moments that now have their own titles – see 'The Shot' and 'The Shot II' – it was a standout moment of inspiration in a career littered with them. On 30 June 1992 in a game against the Portland Trail Blazers, Jordan began by scoring a tasty 35 points in the first half, adding another four to help the Bulls breeze past the Blazers 122-89. By the end of the game, Jordan had hit six three-pointers to send the crowd into raptures. He was on fire, and the now-iconic nonchalant response suggested that even the man himself couldn't quite comprehend his performance.

## THE 1988 DUNK CONTEST

**08** Basketball is all about exhibition, and what better stage to perform on than a dunking competition in front of the world?

Dunking competitions were nothing new when Jordan joined the 1988 event during the All-Star weekend, but with the Bulls forming into one of the most formidable teams in the NBA, everyone was excited to see His Airness step up. Taking place in Chicago, Jordan definitely had the home crowd – and potentially a couple of the judges – on his side. But there could be few complaints when he won with a scorching leap and dunk from the free throw line.

"BY THE END OF THE GAME, JORDAN HAD HIT SIX THREE-POINTERS TO SEND THE CROWD INTO RAPTURES"

# NBA LEGENDS

## NAMED NBA FINALS MVP THREE YEARS STRAIGHT

**09** Once Chicago won their first NBA title in 1991, the seal had been proverbially broken. A new age had begun, and the Bulls were the new kings of American basketball.

For three straight years the they battled their way to the final round of the NBA Finals, and along the way one. Michael Jordan became the only player to be named NBA Finals MVP three times before 1993. During a legendary six-game series against the Phoenix Suns in 1993, Jordan averaged 41 points per game, as the Bulls stormed their way to a three-peat.

## THAT DUNK OVER PATRICK EWING

**10** If you're going to make a dunk heard around the world, why not do it over the head of one of the league's most dominant centres?

That's exactly what Jordan did when the Bulls faced the New York Knicks in the 1991 Eastern Conference finals. Just before the Bulls would go onto to dismiss the Bad Boys of the Detroit Pistons, they needed to get past their other rivals, the dominant Knicks.

Taking place in the final seconds of the first half, Jordan's viciously hard dunk towered over the seven-foot Ewing and helped reduce the Knicks' lead at the time to just two points. Much like Scottie Pippen's dunk over Ewing a couple of years previously, the move summed up the intense rivalry burning in the Eastern Conference in the early 1990s. It's also Jordan's personal favourite dunk.

> "THE MOVE SUMMED UP THE INTENSE RIVALRY"

## CLAIMING THE NCAA TITLE AS A FRESHMAN

**11** Before Jordan claimed double Olympic gold and six NBA titles, he was carving a name for himself in collegiate basketball history.

It wasn't an impact he took his time to make either. During his freshman season, Jordan helped take North Carolina to NCAA championship greatness in 1982. Under coach Dean Smith, Jordan had 13.4 points per game with a 53.4% shooting average. He tore North Carolina's opponents to shreds and saw the college take its first national title in a quarter of a century.

## WINNING THE FIRST RING

**12** By the time Jordan and the Bulls began the 1990-91 season, the Chicago-based franchise had yet to clinch a championship in its 25 years of existence.

But there was something shifting in the Eastern Conference – the LA Lakers were slipping from their perch and the brutality of the Detroit Pistons had lost its edge. Jordan and the Bulls came out swinging, their dismissal of the Pistons in the conference finals setting up a showdown with the Lakers. And while the series wasn't quite the event everyone was hoping for, Jordan put on a masterclass and helped claim Chicago's first NBA title.

## LEADING THE DREAM TEAM

**13** How do you top winning gold at the 1984 Olympics? You go ahead and do it again eight years later at the 1992 games in Barcelona.

In 1984, Jordan had barely been drafted by the Bulls, but at the beginning of the 1990s he had cemented himself as a legend in the making and joined a Team USA filled with fellow icons. Dubbed the 'Dream Team', MJ was flanked by Patrick Ewing, Scottie Pippen, Charles Barkley, John Stockton, Karl Malone, Chris Mullin, David Robinson, Larry Bird and Magic Johnson. Together, Olympic gold was assured and the team became the stuff of legend.

> "DUBBED THE 'DREAM TEAM', MJ WAS FLANKED BY PATRICK EWING, SCOTTIE PIPPEN, CHARLES BARKLEY, LARRY BIRD AND MAGIC JOHNSON TO NAME A FEW"

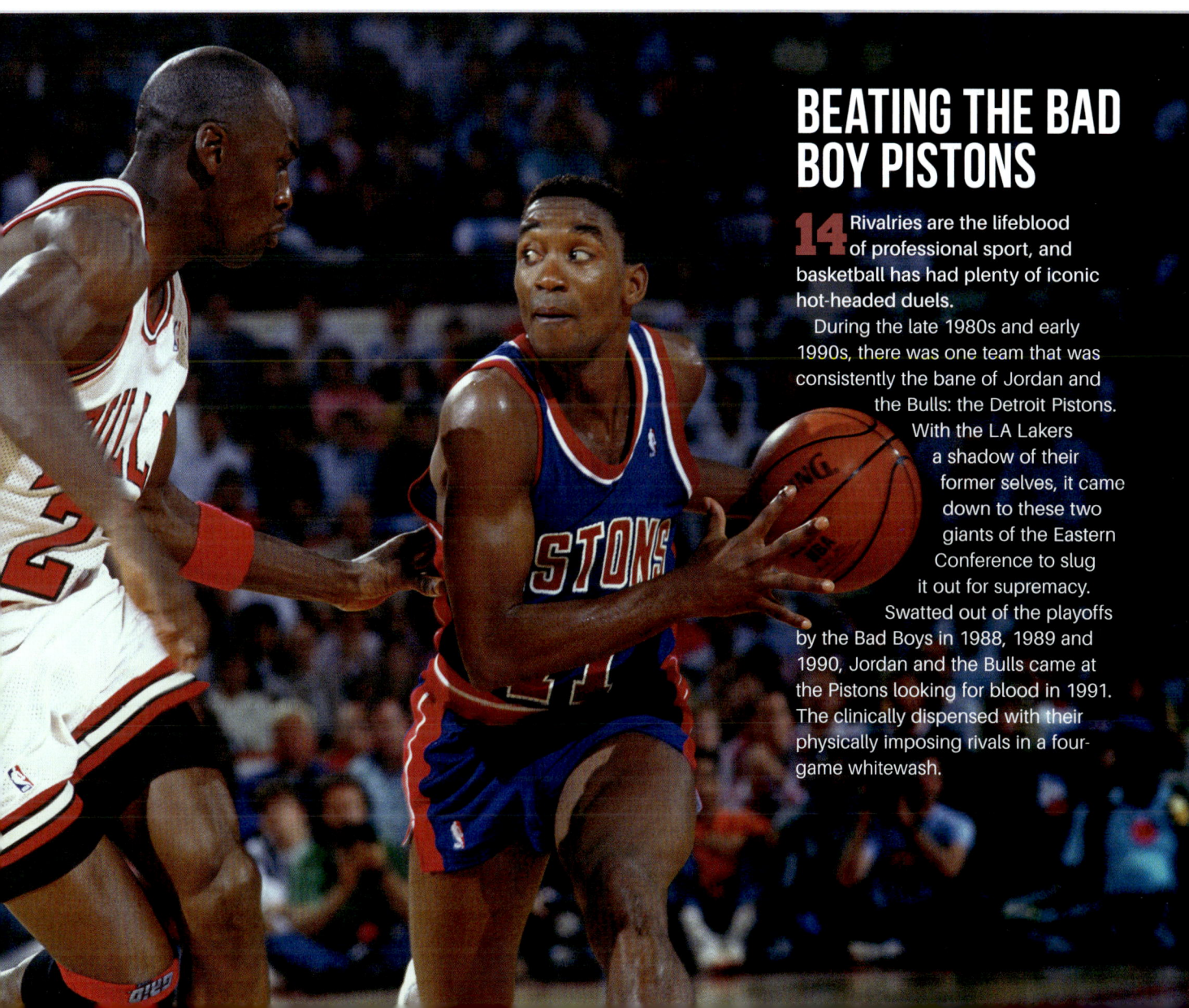

## BEATING THE BAD BOY PISTONS

**14** Rivalries are the lifeblood of professional sport, and basketball has had plenty of iconic hot-headed duels.

During the late 1980s and early 1990s, there was one team that was consistently the bane of Jordan and the Bulls: the Detroit Pistons. With the LA Lakers a shadow of their former selves, it came down to these two giants of the Eastern Conference to slug it out for supremacy. Swatted out of the playoffs by the Bad Boys in 1988, 1989 and 1990, Jordan and the Bulls came at the Pistons looking for blood in 1991. The clinically dispensed with their physically imposing rivals in a four-game whitewash.

# NBA LEGENDS

## BAGGING A 72-WIN SEASON

**15** Ask any basketball fan worth their salt to name the best NBA team of all time and there's a very good chance the words '1995-1996 Chicago Bulls' will tumble from their mouth with awestruck reverence.

That legendary Bulls team was truly a force of nature, and with Jordan at the fore they racked up an unprecedented 72 wins on their way to reclaiming the NBA title after a two-year hiatus from the finals. The previous record of 69 wins, held by the 1970-71 LA Lakers, was smashed when Jordan and the Bulls pulled off an impressive win to down the Milwaukee Bucks on 16 April. The Bulls' mark would stand for two decades until a Stephen Curry-led Golden State Warriors notched 73 wins in 2015-16

## OLYMPIC GOLD IN 1984

**17** In the summer of 1984, Jordan had barely been drafted by the Chicago Bulls (technically he was still a college player at the time) when he was selected for another incredible honour – joining the USA's national basketball team at the 1984 summer Olympics in Los Angeles.

Jordan wasn't the only hyped young player on the team either, with Patrick Ewing, Sam Perkins, Chris Mullin, Steve Alford, and Wayman Tisdale also filling out the ranks with plenty of star power. Still, the young MJ wasn't to be pushed to the sideline, and he led the scoring for Team USA, averaging a cool 17.1 points per game as he and his fellow players steamrollered their way to Olympic gold on home soil. Coached by the legendary Bobby Knight, the win in LA was the first salvo in a pro career where Jordan would win every major accolade out there.

> **"THAT LEGENDARY BULLS TEAM WAS A FORCE OF NATURE, WITH JORDAN AT THE FORE"**

## ROOKIE OF THE YEAR

**16** There was little surprise when Michael Jordan bagged the Rookie of the Year award in his debut season in the NBA.

This was the young man that had effectively led Team USA to Olympic gold just before the season started, lest we forget. And the accolade wasn't awarded on simple goodwill – Jordan earned it with a truly impressive opening year in pro basketball. With the number 23 Bulls jersey on his back, he helped Chicago improve its record to 38-44 and breach the postseason for the first time since 1981. He averaged 28.2 points per game and even earned a place on the All-Star team.

# 23 REASONS JORDAN IS THE GREATEST

## A HIGH OF 69 AGAINST THE CAVS

**18** Michael Jordan has so many records to his name, ranging from points scored to number of shots blocked (his stellar defensive contributions to the Bulls are often overlooked), but his record high of 69 points in a game against the Cleveland Cavaliers in 1990 really stands out.

During the 1989-90 season, the Bulls and the Cavs were headed in two very different directions. While the Bulls were racking up the wins, their Cleveland rivals were slipping further out of contention. So when Jordan racked up a staggering 69 points and an equally jaw-dropping 18 rebounds in a single game on 28 March 1990 it sent a clear message to the Cavs and the rest of the NBA: you're good, but you're not Bulls good.

> "IT SENT A CLEAR MESSAGE TO THE CAVS AND THE REST OF THE NBA: YOU'RE GOOD, BUT YOU'RE NOT BULLS GOOD"

## THE 30K CLUB

**20** More so than in most sports, statistics are integral to basketball.

From points to assists, those all-important numbers don't just win championships, they cement the status of the NBA's elite players. Perhaps the holy grail of stat categories is the fabled '30,000 Point Club', a prestigious group of NBA legends who have accumulated a staggering number of points throughout their careers.

Only five players hold the honour and, hardly surprisingly, Jordan is one of them. He entered the club in third place on 4 January 2002 while wearing a Wizards Jersey.

## 'THE SHOT II'

**19** There aren't many players who pull off a play that passes into sporting myth.

Fewer still manage it twice. But that's the territory of one Michael Jeffrey Jordan. The second, but no less famous basket that has since been immortalised as 'The Shot II', was taken in the 1993 Eastern Conference semi-finals. Once again lined up against the Cleveland Cavaliers, the game had come down to a tie. With mere seconds left on the clock, Jordan charged in and took a shot at the elbow to clinch the game and continue the Bulls' dominance of the Cavs in the 1990s.

> "WITH SECONDS LEFT ON THE CLOCK, JORDAN CHARGED IN AND TOOK A SHOT AT THE ELBOW TO CLINCH THE GAME"

# NBA LEGENDS

## BECOMING A BRAND WITH JUMPMAN

**21** Today, there are plenty of sportsmen and women who enjoy sponsorship deals and agreements with some of the biggest sportswear brands in the world, but very few have ever transcended their sport so completely that they create their own brand.

In 1997, in a landmark partnership with sportswear and shoemaker giant Nike, Jordan did just that. And so, the Jumpman was born. It's a testament to the staying power of that brand that the words 'Air Jordan' are as still as synonymous with Nike as its iconic swoosh. All the more so when you consider that, according to Forbes, the Jumpman brand brings in an annual haul of $1 billion, while occupying over 70% of the lucrative basketball wear market.

## THE FIRST TRIPLE-DOUBLE

**22** MJ wracked up an impressive 28 triple-doubles (three double-digit scores in one of five categories – points, rebounds, steals, assists and blocked shots), but his first as a pro came in 1985 with his most iconic associated team, the Bulls.

In a tense match-up against the Denver Nuggets on 14 January, Jordan scored a total of 35 points, bagged himself 14 rebounds and was on hand to offer a game-changing 15 assists to see another crucial win notched up for the Bulls.

> "IN A TENSE MATCH-UP AGAINST THE NUGGETS, JORDAN SCORED 35 POINTS"

## TAKING OVER HOLLYWOOD WITH SPACE JAM

**23** No list of MJ's greatest achievements can leave out his star turn opposite the cast of *Looney Tunes* in the 1996 blockbuster hit *Space Jam*.

Okay, Jordan was a little wooden in places, and to say it wasn't a hit with critics would be an understatement, but with a final box office gross of $230.4 million against a still hefty (for the time) $80 million budget, *Space Jam* crushed everything else that hit cinema screens upon its release.

Interestingly, *Space Jam* wasn't a Looney Tunes film that happened to include Jordan. Rather, the whole project was created as a vehicle to capatalise on his worldwide image and brand. The film struggled behind the scenes, but Jordan's presence provided the x-factor it needed to reach astronomical cinematic success. The long-rumoured sequel, *Space Jam 2*, with the new global superstar LeBron James in the hotseat, is set to be released in 2021.

# ...AND 5 REASONS HE ISN'T

**It's borderline blasphemous to name anyone other than Michael Jordan as the greatest NBA player of all time, but there are others who have a legitimate claim to the title**

## KAREEM ABDUL-JABBAR

From 1969 to 1989, Kareem Abdul-Jabbar was a phenomenon in the NBA. A king of consistency for 20 seasons, he maintained an incredible level of level of performance over the years. Add to that six NBA titles and the lofty position as leading scorer in NBA history and you've got a pure NBA legend.

## LARRY BIRD

Another basketball icon who made his name during the era that Michael Jordan was emerging, Larry Bird is a living Boston Celtics legend. While Bird was never known for his athleticism per se, he had incredible ball skills, impeccable court awareness and a jump shot that consistently tore the league's meanest defences to shreds. Not to mention his three NBA championship rings.

## BILL RUSSELL

A name often overlooked in favour of Wilt Chamberlain, Kareem Abdul-Jabbar and Michael Jordan himself, Bill Russell is, in terms of titles, the most successful player in the history of the NBA. With 11 NBA rings to his name, and five regular season MVP accolades, Russell remains the greatest defender to ever take to the court. He dogged offensive players from 1956 to 1969 and became a Boston Celtics legend.

## MAGIC JOHNSON

As Jordan was helping build the strength and status of the Bulls in the mid-to-late 1980s, one man was ruling the courts with the LA Lakers: Magic Johnson. With five NBA titles and countless other honours, the 6'9" point guard helped cement the Lakers as the juggernauts of 1980s basketball.

## LEBRON JAMES

Whether playing for the Miami Heat, his hometown Cleveland Cavaliers, or the legendary LA Lakers, LeBron James is the biggest name currently playing in the NBA. James already has three championships to his name, and with his dextrous skill in both offense and defense, it's likely his star will continue to ascend.

# NBA LEGENDS

# LIVING THE DREAM

## RISING FROM OBSCURITY TO COLLEGE STARDOM, HAKEEM OLAJUWON REDEFINED THE ROLE OF AN NBA BIG MAN IN THE 1980s AND 1990s

Growing up in Lagos, Nigeria, Hakeem Olajuwon never dreamed of NBA stardom when he was a kid. In fact, he didn't even start playing basketball until he was 17 years old. Up until then, he had been a goalkeeper in a youth soccer team in Lagos. But when he was encouraged to enter a local basketball tournament, things immediately started moving very quickly for the fast-growing Olajuwon.

He quickly picked up the skills to play basketball at a high level, and his training as a goalkeeper stood him in good stead when it came to footwork, positioning, agility and strength as a basketball player.

Only a year later, he emigrated to the United States, and was invited to try out for the basketball team at the University of Houston, after their coach, Guy Lewis, was tipped off by a friend who had seen Olajuwon play. He got on the team, but didn't get clearance by the NCAA in time to play the first season. He patiently worked on his skills, and played well in a reserve role during his sophomore year at the university, averaging 8.3 points and 6.2 rebounds per game. In the summer of 1982, he received personal tutelage from the Houston Rockets' dominant center Moses Malone, the league's reigning MVP at the time. He went toe to toe with Malone in training and exhibition games that summer, and for the next two years, he developed into a powerful defensive enforcer for his college. By the time his senior year was up, his stock had risen so high that he was selected first overall in the 1984 NBA draft, ahead of budding superstars like Michael Jordan and Charles Barkley. Fittingly, the team that drafted him was the Houston Rockets, where he was tipped to complement reigning Rookie of the Year Ralph Sampson, another tall center with immense athletic ability.

Olajuwon rose incredibly quickly to the challenge of NBA basketball, scoring 24 points in his first-ever game, less than five years after picking up a basketball for the first time. He continued to shine throughout the first season, averaging over 20 points per game, along with 11.9 rebounds and 2.7 blocks per game. He came second in the voting for Rookie of the Year that year, behind only Michael Jordan, and the Rockets improved greatly. Having only won 29 games in 1983-84, Houston won 48 in Olajuwon's first season and made it to the playoffs, where they lost narrowly to Utah Jazz in the first round.

Olajuwon's background as a soccer goalkeeper helped his timing, agility and balance as a defensive force in basketball

## HAKEEM OLAJUWON

**POSITION:** Center
**NBA DRAFT:** 1984/Round 1/Pick 1
**CAREER:** Houston Rockets (1984-2001), Toronto Raptors (2001-2002)

### HIGHLIGHTS:
2x NBA Champion (1994, 1995)
1x NBA MVP (1994)
2x NBA Finals MVP (1994, 1995)
12x All-Star Team (1985-1990, 1992-1997)
12x All-NBA Team (1986-1991, 1993-1997, 1999)
2x Defensive Player of the Year (1993, 1994)
5x All-Defensive First Team (1987, 1988, 1990, 1993, 1994)
3x NBA blocks leader (1990, 1991, 1993)
2x NBA rebounding leader (1989, 1990)

### STATS:
**REGULAR SEASON**
Points: 26,946 | Rebounds: 13,748 | Blocks: 3,830

**PLAYOFFS**
Points: 3,755 | Rebounds: 1,621 | Blocks: 472

HAKEEM OLAJUWON

"HE WAS SELECTED FIRST OVERALL IN THE 1984 NBA DRAFT, AHEAD OF BUDDING SUPERSTARS LIKE MICHAEL JORDAN AND CHARLES BARKLEY"

Hakeem Olajuwon rose quickly to fame and ultimately became one of the greatest centers in NBA history

# NBA LEGENDS

Olajuwon (left) and fellow seven-footer Ralph Sampson brought the Rockets back to title contention during the mid-1980s

> **"IN 1993-94, OLAJUWON IMPROVED HIS PLAY EVEN FURTHER, AVERAGING 27.3 POINTS PER GAME ON THE WAY TO HIS FIRST MVP AWARD"**

Further improvement followed; the next season Olajuwon was already outshining Sampson, averaging 23.5 points, 11.5 rebounds and 3.4 blocks per game on the way to 51 wins. Even bigger success followed in the playoffs, where the Rockets broke the Los Angeles Lakers' monopoly of the Western Conference with a shock upset in the Conference Finals. Olajuwon averaged 31 points per game in a 4-1 series win, where the Lakers simply couldn't contain him, despite double and triple-teaming him throughout the series. In the Finals, they gave the Boston Celtics a good run for their money before finally succumbing in six games, where Olajuwon once again led the way with 24.8 points and 11.8 rebounds per game. The Rockets seemed poised to supplant the Lakers as a dominant force in the West for years to come. However, injuries would intervene, albeit not to Olajuwon himself, but his 'Twin Towers' counterpart, the 7-feet 4-inches tall Sampson.

Limited to only 43 games during the 1986-87 season, Sampson couldn't help Olajuwon's Rockets as he did the year before. The team only won 42 games in the regular season, and got knocked out in the second round of the playoffs. The following season, Sampson was traded to the Golden State Warriors, and an increasingly frustrated Olajuwon didn't receive enough support from the Rockets front office to repeat the success of 1986's Finals run. Despite fantastic individual seasons, where Olajuwon twice led the league in rebounding and twice in blocked shots, he didn't have the supporting cast to get beyond the first round of the playoffs for the next four straight seasons. Things eventually reached a nadir in 1991-92, when injuries limited Olajuwon early in the season, and the Rockets failed to make the playoffs altogether.

Fed up with the lack of support from the team's owners, Olajuwon demanded a trade in the summer of 1992, and was close to being shipped out before Rudy Tomjanovich entered as a new coach and convinced him to stay. Under Tomjanovich, Olajuwon started to focus more on his passing, and averaged a career-high 3.5 assists per game in 1992-93. This in turn opened up scoring opportunities for him, as teams couldn't simply throw bodies at him now he had improved his skill at finding teammates when double or triple-teamed in the post. That season, he averaged a career-high 26.1 points per game, topped off with a Defensive Player of the Year award and a trip to the Western Conference Semifinals, where the Rockets narrowly lost to the Seattle Supersonics in a thrilling seven-game series. That post-season, Olajuwon managed the remarkable feat of leading his team in scoring, rebounding, assists, steals and blocks, something he would repeat a year later on an even more successful playoffs run.

In 1993-94, Olajuwon improved his play even further, averaging 27.3 points per game on the way to his first MVP award, and a post-season run that took him all the way to the Finals, where he would face off with his longtime rival, the New York Knicks' star center Patrick Ewing. In a physically grinding seven-game series, Olajuwon proved the difference-maker. Scoring almost 27 points per game, he held Ewing, who had been on a tear up until the playoffs, to only 18.9 points per game in the series, and only 17 points in the deciding Game 7. It had taken a decade, but Hakeem Olajuwon had delivered Houston its first-ever NBA title. Not only that, but Olajuwon became the first player in history to win the title and the MVP, Finals MVP and Defensive Player of the Year awards in the same season. But Hakeem and the Rockets were far from sated.

The 1994-95 season started brightly, with the Rockets

Few players could rival Olajuwon at the post, partly thanks to his excellent footwork

Olajuwon goes up against the Utah Jazz's Karl Malone in the 1994 playoffs

## HAKEEM OLAJUWON

## A QUADRUPLE-TRIPLE THREAT

**FOUR PLAYERS HAVE RECORDED A QUADRUPLE-DOUBLE IN THE NBA. ONLY OLAJUWON HAS DONE IT TWICE**

Even though we see it more frequently today, a triple-double remains a major achievement. But an even bigger achievement is the elusive quadruple-double, as reaching double figures in four of the five major counting stats (points, rebounds, assists, steals and blocks) is a near-impossible task for any NBA player.

In the NBA's history, only four players have achieved this; Nate Thurmond in 1974, Alvin Robertson in 1986, Olajuwon in 1990 and David Robinson in 1994.

What makes Olajuwon's feat more impressive is that he did this twice in the same month. On 3 March 1990, Olajuwon tallied 29 points, 18 rebounds, 10 assists and 11 blocks against the Golden State Warriors, and then he repeated the feat on 29 March against the Milwaukee Bucks, whipping up 18 points, 16 rebounds, 10 assists and 11 blocks. It should not come as a surprise that he led the league in blocks that season, with 376 in total. Only Mark Eaton and Manute Bol had topped that before, and no player has matched Olajuwon's 1989–90 tally since.

Olajuwon was perhaps the best rim protector the modern NBA has seen

winning their nine opening games, but they only won 38 of the 73 remaining regular season games, even with superstar Clyde Drexler joining from Portland at the trade deadline in February and Olajuwon improving his scoring even further to 27.8 points per game. However, showing true grit, the Rockets ground their way through the star-studded Western Conference playoffs, beating the Karl Malone-led Utah Jazz 3-2, the Charles Barkley-led Phoenix Suns 4-3 and David Robinson's San Antonio Spurs 4-2 to reach the Finals again. This time, the team awaiting them was Orlando Magic, a much younger team led by regular-season scoring champion Shaquille O'Neal. However, the vast gap in experience showed, as the Rockets swept the series 4-0 where Finals MVP Olajuwon dominated Shaq throughout, averaging 32.8 points, 11.5 rebounds and 5.5 assists in the series.

Dreams of a three-peat would come to nought, however, as the Rockets were swept by the SuperSonics in the 1996 Western Conference Finals. Despite adding Charles Barkley and Olajuwon still averaging 23-plus points in 1996–97, the Rockets again failed to make the Finals, losing to the Utah Jazz in the Western Conference Finals. The following year, Olajuwon's production started to drop, and with it the Rockets chance to contend for the title drifted away. Now nagged by persistent injuries, Olajuwon never played more than 58 games in a season for the ageing Rockets as they headed for a rebuild. As part of this rebuild, Olajuwon himself was traded to the Toronto Raptors for the 2001–02 season, where he played one final season before retiring after an illustrious 18-year career. Hakeem Olajuwon retired as the NBA's all-time leader in blocks, a record he still holds today.

After leaving college, Chamberlain played for the Harlem Globetrotters for a season, alongside the legendary Meadowlark Lemon

# RISE OF THE BIG DIPPER

**THE GIANT CENTER RACKED UP RECORD SCORES LIKE NO PLAYER BEFORE OR SINCE – AND WILL BE REMEMBERED FOREVER FOR ONE MYTHICAL NIGHT IN PENNSYLVANIA**

Wilt Chamberlain's career stats are simply not to be believed. There have been dominant basketball players before and since, but the 7-foot 1-inch giant was in a class of his own.

The late Hall of Famer still boasts each of the top four scoring seasons in points per game in NBA history – and five of the top six. Indeed, in his 1961-62 season for the Philadelphia Warriors, Chamberlain scored on average more than 50 points a game. For your typical All-Star – never mind a member of the NBA's rank and file – scoring 50 points in any one game would be a career highlight.

Coming straight into the league, Chamberlain scored 37.6 points per game – which was better than even Michael Jordan at the peak of his powers. It was impressive enough to convince the voters to name the 23-year-old the NBA MVP straight off the bat (and, of course, Rookie of the Year too).

Over the course of his glittering professional career, which spanned 1959 until 1973, Wilt Chamberlain scored a scarcely believable 30.1 points per game. He currently sits seventh on the all-time points scored list above legends like Shaquille O'Neal, Moses Malone, Tim Duncan and Kevin Garnett. Five of the six players who have surpassed him – Kareem Abdul-Jabbar, Karl Malone, LeBron James, Kobe Bryant and Dirk Nowitzki – played significantly more than Chamberlain's 1,045 career games.

The one who didn't – Michael Jordan – matched Wilt's lifetime 30.1 points per game. The deeper one delves into his career the further one's jaw drops. He won four NBA MVP titles – an accomplishment only bettered by Abdul-Jabbar, Jordan and Chamberlain's great nemesis, Bill Russell.

The man they called 'the Big Dipper' was also selected for the All-Star game 13 times, led the league in scoring seven times and in rebounds 11 times. In his penultimate season, he won the NBA Finals MVP with the Los Angeles Lakers. Such was the magnitude of his achievements that three separate franchises – the Golden State Warriors, Philadelphia 76ers and the Lakers – retired forever his famous number 13 jersey. But none of the aforementioned achievements hold a candle to Chamberlain's greatest feat – scoring 100 points in a single basketball game against the New York Knicks in 1962.

So, in light of all of the above, why isn't Chamberlain more widely considered basketball's GOAT (Greatest Of All Time)? There are myriad reasons for this apparent omission. Some are legitimate, technical factors, providing qualification or context to his greatness. Others are wrapped up in his often-abrasive character, or his shortcomings as a teammate and a collector of silverware.

Of course, there are many serious scholars of the sport who consider Chamberlain second only to Michael Jordan. Indeed, former greats, such as Scottie Pippen, Walt Frazier and Rick Barry, consider him the best of all.

There are several mitigating factors to some of Chamberlain's gaudier numbers. First, the pace of professional basketball was much greater in Chamberlain's day – when sides typically had about 25 per cent more possessions each game. The more

# WILT CHAMBERLAIN

Wilt Chamberlain (no 13) goes up to the rim despite pressure from his great rival, the Boston Celtics' Bill Russell (no 6)

Wilt Chamberlain (no 13), then playing for the Los Angeles Lakers, faced off against the Celtics in the 1969 NBA finals

## WILT CHAMBERLAIN

**POSITION:** Center
**NBA DRAFT:** 1959/Territorial pick
**CAREER:** Philadelphia/San Francisco Warriors (1959-1965), Philadelphia 76ers (1965-1968), Los Angeles Lakers (1968-1973)

### HIGHLIGHTS:
2x NBA Champion (1967, 1972)
1x NBA Finals MVP (1972)
4x NBA MVP (1960, 1966-1968)
13x NBA All-Star Team (1960-1969, 1971-1973)
1x All-Star MVP (1960)
1x NBA Rookie of the Year (1960)
10x All-NBA Team (1960-1968, 1972)
7x NBA scoring champion (1960-1966)
11x NBA rebounding champion (1960-1963, 1966-1969, 1971-1973)
1x NBA assists leader (1968)

### STATS:
**REGULAR SEASON**
Points: 31,419 | Rebounds: 23,924 | Assists: 4,643

**PLAYOFFS**
Points: 3,607 | Rebounds: 3,913 | Assists: 673

chances you have to score, the higher your numbers should be. It's also true that the NBA of the 1960s was virtually tailor-made for his exact strengths. Because there was no three-point line, fashioning shots close to the rim was of paramount importance. Likewise, taking rebounds close to the rim was more common – because more players were taking shots closer in. His height and strength were ideally suited to these conditions, while his Achilles' heel – shooting from further than five feet – was far less critical than it is today.

Chamberlain is also downgraded in people's minds because his haul of two NBA titles is dwarfed by Bill Russell's 11. While

## NBA LEGENDS

he may have been a more gifted athlete than his great rival, he was never able to get the best of the legendary Boston Celtics teams of the 1960s.

Born in Philadelphia in 1936, Wilt was one of nine children. By the age of ten, he had reportedly grown to around 6-feet tall – and was a gigantic 6-feet 11-inches by the time he entered Overbrook High School. After winning a clutch of local city championships, he was snapped up by the University of Kansas. An athlete of supreme gifts, the young man quickly developed a reputation for his deceptive grace and economy of movement – as well as his obvious height and strength.

After being named an All-American in 1957 and 1958, Wilt left college prematurely, electing to spend a year with the Harlem Globetrotters, the world-famous exhibition team.

Playing alongside the celebrated Meadowlark Lemon, Chamberlain was adopted as a member of the iconic showboaters at the dawn of the team's heyday. He was a member of the squad which travelled to the Soviet Union in 1959.

Entering the NBA draft, Chamberlain was taken by the Philadelphia Warriors – the precursor to today's Golden State team – with a Territorial pick. He would go on to break countless records with the team, averaging 41.6 point a game through his first five seasons in the league. It was during this time that Chamberlain and Russell would start to forge a fiercely competitive relationship on the court and a close one off it – for the time being, at least.

The big Philadelphian made an instant impact on a league which had never before seen a player with his physical gifts. Even among the other centers of the day, he towered over the competition. In his first game in the NBA, away to the New York Knicks, Chamberlain scored 43 points and made 28 rebounds in a 118-109 win. He would follow it up two games later with 41 points and 40 rebounds against the Syracuse Nationals. Chamberlain was just four games into his pro career before meeting Bill Russell's Boston Celtics – who would prove to be his bête noire in his playing days.

In a sign of things to come, the Celtics would run out 115-106 winners – even though Chamberlain outscored Russell. Despite the setback, Wilt would continue to put in commanding performances in virtually all the games he played in, averaging 37.6 points per game as the Warriors went 49-26.

The Celtics would come back to haunt Philadelphia in the playoffs, though, eliminating them in the Eastern Division Finals in six games. Boston's dominance would continue in the coming years, winning the NBA championship each year for the next six years.

Although he would not win a title with the Warriors, the crowning moment of Chamberlain's career came in March 1962, midway through his most impressive statistical year. In an untelevised game in Hershey, Pennsylvania, Chamberlain scored an unprecedented 100 points in a game.

No one inside the arena that night could believe what they had witnessed – as Chamberlain brutalised his opponents.

Pictured in his high school days, Chamberlain was gifted with a blend of height, strength and agility

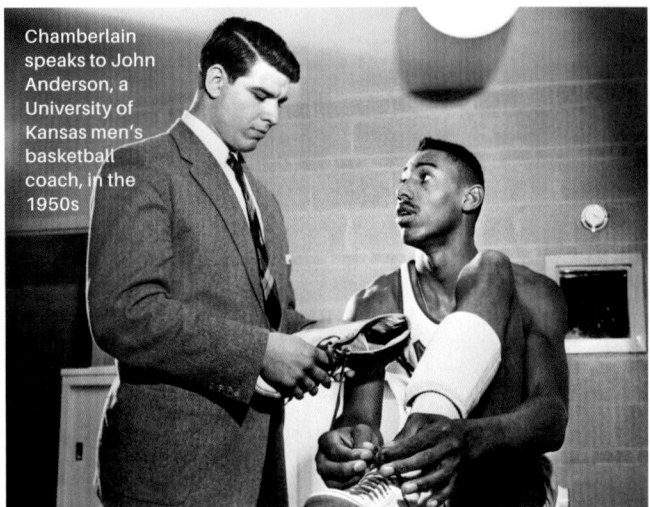

Chamberlain speaks to John Anderson, a University of Kansas men's basketball coach, in the 1950s

No basketball player has since even come close to replicating the feat. The most celebrated individual performance of recent decades – Kobe Bryant's virtually perfect masterclass against the Toronto Raptors in 2006 – fell 19 points short. Chamberlain would be a Warrior for the next three seasons – albeit now in the San Francisco Bay Area, after the team was relocated.

He was soon back in his Philly, though – being traded to the 76ers during the 1965 All-Star break. He found himself on a team packed full of talent. Chamberlain won his second MVP award in the 1965-66 season but was again eliminated from postseason contention by the epochal Celtics team. He would be named the league's best player in each of the next two seasons, too.

The 1966-67 season brought Chamberlain his first championship, when Philadelphia became the first side to win a playoff series against Boston since 1958, downing the Celtics 4-1.

Facing off against his former team, the San Francisco Warriors, the legendary center led the 76ers to a rousing 4-2 series win to clinch the crown. Chamberlain later switched to the West Coast, moving to the Los Angeles Lakers, the NBA's most glamorous franchise, in 1968. The big man's legacy was cemented when, playing alongside Jerry West, he was crowned NBA champion for the second time in 1972. The 4-1 decimation of the New York Knicks also saw Chamberlain named Finals MVP.

Chamberlain playing for the LA Lakers, goes up for a layup against the Chicago Bulls in 1972

# WILT CHAMBERLAIN

## THE 100-POINT GAME

### CHAMBERLAIN SCORED AN UNMATCHED AND UNPRECEDENTED 100 POINTS

For all his championships and personal records, to this day Wilt Chamberlain is best known for his 100-point game in the 1961-62 season.

Shooting an efficient 36 for 63 from the floor, it was by far the greatest scoring night in the history of professional basketball. The famously erratic free-throw shooter even scored 28 of 32 from the line in the Philadelphia Warriors' 169-147 victory over the New York Knicks.

He had already played a couple of 70-plus point games – scoring 78 against the Los Angeles Lakers on 8 December 1961 and then 73 the following January against the Chicago Packers. The only other man to come close to that level of scoring was Kobe Bryant, who scored 81 in 2006.

But on 2 March 1962, Chamberlain found himself in the zone. Everything the Warriors did was focused towards getting the ball into his hands, and everything he tried came off.

No television cameras were present on the night, and the lack of surviving footage only adds to the mystique of the night. Even more than 50 years on, it is still comfortably the best statistical night any player has ever experienced – and one of the greatest sporting performances of the 20th century. It's a record that will likely never be broken.

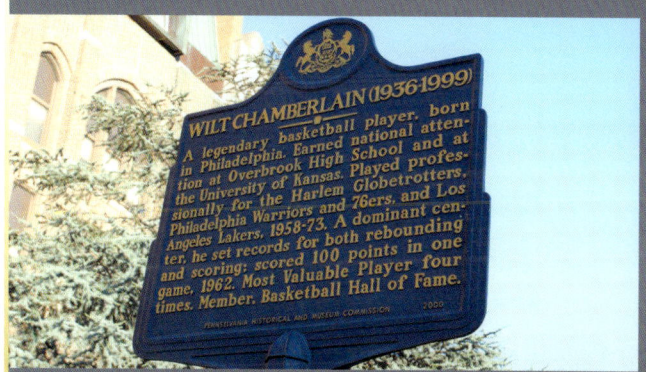

An historical plaque outside Overbrook High School commemorates Chamberlain's career and his incredible 100-point game

Chamberlain was famed for his size and strength, although he was consistently derided for his poor free-throw shooting

Since hanging up his jersey in 1973, Chamberlain has gone down in NBA history as one of the most dominating physical presences in all of basketball – if not all sports.

The towering center may not have been loved in his time, but he certainly was universally feared. Even though the game has changed beyond recognition in the intervening years, Wilt Chamberlain's achievements and myriad records have seldom been matched.

*"CHAMBERLAIN HAS GONE DOWN IN NBA HISTORY AS ONE OF THE MOST DOMINATING PHYSICAL PRESENCES IN ALL OF BASKETBALL – IF NOT ALL SPORTS"*

# NBA LEGENDS

Julius Erving, pictured playing for the Philadelphia 76ers, helped to introduce modern flair to professional basketball

# THE HIGH-FLYING PIONEER

**FEW MEN HAVE INFLUENCED BASKETBALL MORE THAN JULIUS ERVING, WHO PIONEERED THE ABOVE-THE-RIM, SLAM-DUNKING STYLE SYNONYMOUS WITH THE NBA TODAY**

If any one man invented the modern game of basketball, it was Julius Erving.

Before starring in the NBA, he was the face of the rival American Basketball Association, hoovering up titles and accolades – first with the Virginia Squires and then the New York Nets. During his time in the ABA, he popularised the three-point shot and dunking and won two titles, three MVPs and two playoff MVP awards.

With the merging of the two leagues came a move to the Philadelphia 76ers, and a greater audience for Erving to showcase his otherworldly skills. He capped his illustrious playing career with an NBA title, an MVP award and a clutch of All-Star appearances, silencing those who accused him of being a flat-track bully in the less prestigious ABA.

Erving has an impressive CV, without doubt and although there are plenty of players out there who have won more silverware, the man they called 'Dr J' is universally considered one of the most important and influential figures to have ever dunked a ball. Erving's influence largely came down to his image and revolutionary playing style. That is not to suggest he was anything other than a superb player – but to weigh his sporting accomplishments alone is to underestimate his impact.

For the last three decades or more, professional basketball has been played with an emphasis on supreme athleticism, especially in leaping and playing above the rim. Basketball is notable among US sports for encouraging innovation and improvisation. It's easy to forget that these elements were not always part of the sport – nor was their introduction inevitable.

First, Erving possessed the rare combination of strength and grace

A young Julius Erving, shortly after signing for his first ABA team, the Virginia Squires

# JULIUS ERVING

**"THE MAN THEY CALLED 'DR J' IS UNIVERSALLY CONSIDERED ONE OF THE MOST IMPORTANT AND INFLUENTIAL FIGURES TO HAVE EVER DUNKED A BALL"**

to pull off these stunning aerial moves. But, more impressively, he had the courage to pioneer them at a time when the NCAA actively banned slam dunks. He was one of the men who shaped the league, which prized the electrifying style exhibited in later decades by Michael Jordan and Kobe Bryant.

And it's no coincidence that Dr J was at the height of his powers in the same decade basketball's popularity skyrocketed. If any NBA star is synonymous with the 1970s, it is Erving.

Born and raised on Long Island, New York, Erving first picked up the 'Dr J' moniker while playing for Roosevelt High School's basketball team. After graduating, he enrolled at the University of Massachusetts in 1968, where he quickly made a name for himself.

Although he averaged 26.3 points and 20 rebounds per game over two seasons, he left the college early to pursue a career in the pro game. While the NBA at the time did not allow teams to draft players less than four years out of high school, the ABA did.

Erving was swiftly scooped up by the Virginia Squires in 1971. In two seasons, the powerful small forward with the distinctive Afro hairstyle became known for his dunking – appearing to some to be walking on air. He became eligible for the NBA draft in 1972 and was picked 12th overall by the Milwaukee Bucks, which would have seen him team up with Oscar Robertson and Kareem Abdul-Jabbar. However, following a messy struggle between the Squires, the Atlanta Hawks and the Bucks over who owned Erving's playing rights, he was traded by the cash-strapped Virginia franchise to the New York Nets in 1973.

It was back in New York where Dr J became a household name. In each of his three seasons with the Nets, he was named ABA MVP, winning the ABA title in 1974 and 1976, overcoming the Utah Stars and Denver Nuggets respectively.

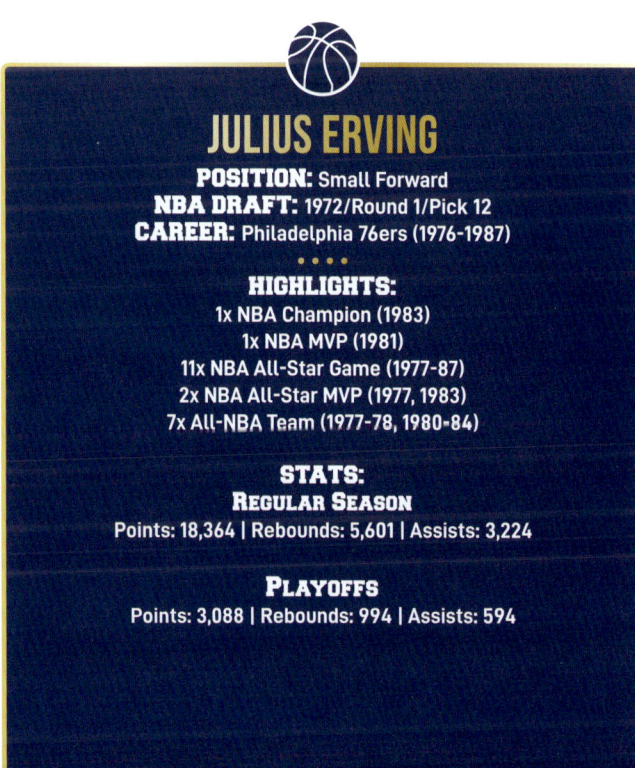

## JULIUS ERVING
**POSITION:** Small Forward
**NBA DRAFT:** 1972/Round 1/Pick 12
**CAREER:** Philadelphia 76ers (1976-1987)

**HIGHLIGHTS:**
1x NBA Champion (1983)
1x NBA MVP (1981)
11x NBA All-Star Game (1977-87)
2x NBA All-Star MVP (1977, 1983)
7x All-NBA Team (1977-78, 1980-84)

**STATS:**
**REGULAR SEASON**
Points: 18,364 | Rebounds: 5,601 | Assists: 3,224

**PLAYOFFS**
Points: 3,088 | Rebounds: 994 | Assists: 594

## DR J'S BASELINE SCOOP MOVE

**ON A COURT FULL OF ALL-STARS IN THE NBA FINALS, ERVING STOLE THE SHOW WITH ONE OF BASKETBALL'S MOST FAMOUS MOVES**

Julius Erving made a career out of logic-defying leaps and acrobatic plays – but his most famous basket came in Game 4 of the 1980 NBA Finals against the vaunted Los Angeles Lakers.

Julius Erving attempts a more conventional shot in 1981

Referred to either as the 'baseline scoop move' or 'reverse lay-up' – or sometimes just as Dr J's 'baseline move' – the winding midair shot left all who witnessed it speechless.

In the fourth quarter of the game, which the Philadelphia 76ers won to level the series 2-2, Erving picked up the ball and ran from the right-hand side towards the rim. Seeing the Lakers' Mark Landsberger approach, he headed towards the baseline until he was behind the basket.

With Kareem Abdul-Jabbar covering the basket under the rim, Dr J leapt into the air, clutching the ball with just the palm of his right hand.

Seeming to hang for an eternity, he then looped his arm down before laying the ball off the backboard and through the hoop, sending the home crowd wild.

Magic Johnson, who was sitting on the bench, later claimed it was the "all-time greatest move I've seen," saying that he appeared to be "walking on air".

Of course, the self-effacing Erving later referred to it as "just another move".

Upon the merger with the NBA, Erving was traded to the Philadelphia 76ers. He was quickly adopted as the face of the franchise, helping the Sixers become one of NBA's best and most popular franchises.

Erving suffered three painful losses in the NBA Finals, including twice to the Los Angeles Lakers of Kareem Abdul-Jabbar and Magic Johnson, as pressure piled on his shoulders to bring a championship to Philadelphia.

After losing the NBA Finals the previous season, Dr J's crowning moment came in the 1982–83 season. In new signing Moses Malone, the reigning MVP, the Sixers found the perfect center to complement Erving. After going 65-17, Philadelphia swept the New York Knicks before besting Milwaukee in five games to set up a Finals against the Lakers.

The 76ers then got their revenge, sweeping their rivals 4-0 to claim Dr J's only NBA trophy, getting the monkey off his back for good.

## NBA LEGENDS

Abdul-Jabbar's iconic skyhook earned him and his team thousands of points over his 20-year NBA career

### KAREEM ABDUL-JABBAR

**POSITION:** Center
**NBA DRAFT:** 1969/Round 1/Pick 1
**CAREER:** Milwaukee Bucks (1969-1975), LA Lakers (1975-1989)

• • • •

#### HIGHLIGHTS:
6x NBA Champion (1971, 1980, 1982, 1985, 1987, 1988)
2x NBA Finals MVP, (1971, 1985)
6x NBA MVP, (1971, 1972, 1974, 1976, 1977, 1980)
19x NBA All-Star Team (1970-77, 1979-1989)
15x All-NBA First Team (1970-74, 1976-81, 1983-86)
5x NBA All-Defensive First Team (1974, 1975, 1979-81)
1x NBA Rookie of the Year (1970)
2x NBA scoring champion (1971, 1972)
1x NBA rebounding champion (1976)
4x NBA blocks leader (1975, 1976, 1979, 1980)

#### STATS:
**REGULAR SEASON**
Points: 38,387 | Rebounds: 17,440 | Blocks: 3,189

**PLAYOFFS**
Points: 5,762 | Rebounds: 2,481 | Blocks: 476

# KAREEM ABDUL-JABBAR

# THE SKYHOOK'S THE LIMIT

## KAREEM ABDUL-JABBAR'S INCREDIBLE STATISTICS ARE JUST A SMALL PART OF WHAT MAKES HIM ONE OF THE NBA'S ALL-TIME LEGENDS

A sportsperson can achieve legendary status in a number of ways. They can top the statistics tables, demonstrating their talent. They can win trophies, proving their worth in a top-quality team. They can be an innovator, taking the game to a new level. They can be a trailblazer outside the sport, forging a new path for others to follow in their wake. Most great sportspeople fit into a couple of these categories. However, it takes a special kind of star, a special kind of talent, a special kind of person to not only fit into all of them, but to be one of the elite in every single category. But, in Kareem Abdul-Jabbar, the world found such a person.

Abdul-Jabbar was born Ferdinand Lewis Alcindor Jr on 16 April 1947 in New York. From school age, his almost freakish height marked him out as a future basketball star.

He joined UCLA Bruins and led them to an unprecedented – though predicted – period of success, at one point going on a 47-game winning streak. In fact, Alcindor was so dominant that, in 1967, the NCAA banned the slam dunk. The ruling would become known as the 'Lew Alcindor rule', as it was believed to have been brought in to counteract the near-impossibility of defending against the 7-foot 2-inch center.

The dunking ban was never going to deter the hard-working and innovative Alcindor, so it was also during his college career that he developed his signature move – the skyhook. Almost more difficult to defend against than the banned slam dunk, Alcindor's technique of getting his body between his marker and the ball, extending his arm skywards and flipping the ball over despairing arms into the net brought even higher levels of fame, notoriety and success.

After an incredibly impressive college career, in which he was named Player of the Year in 1967 and 1969, Alcindor was the number one draft in 1969 – going to the Milwaukee Bucks, who had won first pick on quite possibly one of the most valuable coin tosses in history. Alcindor led the team to second place in

# NBA LEGENDS

the division, eventually losing out to the New York Knicks in the Conference Finals. Alcindor may not have got a championship ring in his debut season but the personal accolades continued to flow. He earned a place on the All-Star team and was named Rookie of the Year for topping the points scoring charts with 2,361.

However, Alcindor didn't have to wait long for that illustrious piece of basketball jewellery to adorn his finger. The very next season Alcindor was a man possessed as the Bucks topped the division, eased through the playoffs and whitewashed the Baltimore Bullets 4-0 in the Finals. Alcindor was named league MVP, Finals MVP and once again came top of the points-scoring table.

During his time at college, he became politically active. He was one of a number of prominent black athletes who met with Muhammad Ali to discuss the boxer's refusal to be drafted for the Vietnam War and chose not to compete for the USA in the 1968 Olympics due to his unease over the way black people were treated in the country. Despite being born into a Catholic family, Alcindor found himself drawn towards the religion of Islam, which offered a way to connect to his African Muslim roots and the inspirational figure of Malcolm X. The day after the Bucks Finals victory he announced his conversion to Islam, changing his name to Kareem Abdul-Jabbar (meaning 'the noble one, servant of the Almighty'). There was a large backlash from the American public who, according to Abdul-Jabbar, didn't know much about Islam and perceived the move as one of the country's biggest sports stars turning his back on America and its values. Abdul-Jabbar stuck to his guns, however, fully committed to his new religion and even married fellow convert Habiba because of a recommendation by his spiritual leader. He did not invite his parents to the wedding, which led to a long-term resentment between them. Abdul-

Abdul-Jabbar won five NBA championships during a dominant period for the Lakers in the 1980s, adding to the one he won with the Bucks

Jabbar and Habiba went on to have three children, but stopped living together in 1973, eventually divorcing in 1978.

Despite the turmoil in his personal life off the court, things continued to go from strength to strength on it. Abdul-Jabbar scored 2,822 points in 1972 – which would prove to be his record highest for a season and the ninth highest of all time –

The combination of Abdul-Jabbar's ruthlessness and Magic Johnson's flair was a devastating one

and won a second straight league MVP award. A third followed in 1974 but Abdul-Jabbar wouldn't win another championship ring while in Milwaukee, losing in the 1972 and 1974 finals. After a poor 1974-75 season, Abdul-Jabbar decided he wanted out. Despite having two years left on his contract, Abdul-Jabbar told the Bucks bosses that he wouldn't be signing another and that he wanted to move somewhere else. As with many aspects of his life, the decision was not so much for the basketball, but more to find somewhere where there were more people that shared his personal beliefs. LA or New York were Abdul-Jabbar's preferred destinations and it was the West that won the day in the end. Abdul-Jabbar was traded to the LA Lakers in exchange for Junior Bridgeman, Dave Meyers, Elmore Smith and Brian Winters ahead of the 1975-76 season.

More personal triumphs followed for Abdul-Jabbar, winning two consecutive league MVP awards in his first two seasons in LA, making it five in seven seasons in the NBA, but that wasn't to translate into team success. The Lakers were thumped 4-0 by Portland Trail Blazers in the 1976-77 Conference Finals, the only time they got past the semifinals in Abdul-Jabbar's first four seasons at the club.

However, all that would change in the 1979-80 season. The Lakers used their first overall pick to select Michigan State point guard Earvin Johnson Jr - better known by his nickname Magic. Abdul-Jabbar and Johnson were to prove an irresistible combination, with Abdul-Jabbar's relentless work rate and dynamic shooting complemented by Johnson's innovation, flair and passing range. The two of them would help the Lakers dominate the season, topping their division and romping to victory in the Finals, beating the Philadelphia 76ers 4-2. Abdul-Jabbar would earn his final league MVP award this year – putting him on six, which remains an all-time NBA record to this day – with Johnson claiming the Finals MVP award. In a reversal of his time at the Bucks, team honours flowed during Abdul-Jabbar's time at the Lakers, while the individual honours dried up. The Lakers reached the NBA Finals in seven of the next eight years, winning four of them in a period of spectacular success, spearheaded by Abdul-Jabbar and Johnson.

As in-sync the combination between Abdul-Jabbar and Johnson was on the court, the pair couldn't have been more different off it. While Johnson was at ease with the media, confident, cocky and the ultimate showman, Abdul-Jabbar was much more reserved. He was perceived as a cold, distant person and preferred reading in the locker room, rather than the usual pre and post-game activities. This may be one of the reasons why, despite his phenomenal stats and achievements, he often isn't one of the first names many people think of when they talk about the greatest NBA players of all time. Names such as Johnson, Jordan, Bryant and James are not only instantly recognisable due to their ability, but because their personalities were so much more media-friendly. Abdul-Jabbar never had that ease with public speaking – something he would later say was one of his biggest regrets.

## KAREEM'S SIGNATURE SKYHOOK

**ABDUL-JABBAR WAS NEVER A MAN TO TAKE A CHALLENGE LYING DOWN – SO IT'S LITTLE SURPRISE HE INVENTED A SHOT TO CONFOUND THE RULE-MAKERS**

Some might say Steph Curry's long three-pointer is the most iconic shot in the game, while others might point to Sarunas Marciulionis's Euro Step. However, if any one player is defined by any one move, it was Kareem Abdul-Jabbar's skyhook. A turn, a leap, a body between ball and opponent, an arm stretched towards the sky, a flick of the wrist and, inevitably, two points.

The skyhook was an unstoppable shot as there was almost no way to defend against it without giving away a foul. Abdul-Jabbar admitted that it was something of an ugly shot, without the grace of an arcing three-pointer or a devastating dunk. However, it was unarguably effective and just part of the reason why Abdul-Jabbar is so far clear at the top of the all-time points scorer list. The fact that it was developed as a direct result of a rule change designed to inhibit Abdul-Jabbar's natural gifts somehow make the success of the shot even sweeter – and the fact the skyhook was the shot that took Abdul-Jabbar ahead of Wilt Chamberlain's record was almost written in the stars.

The skyhook represented Abdul-Jabbar in so many ways. Relentless, accurate, uncompromising, effective without a care for style, the skyhook and Kareem Abdul-Jabbar were a match made in heaven.

A brutal combination of factors meant that Kareem Abdul-Jabbar's skyhook couldn't be defended – all because of a no-dunking college rule

# NBA LEGENDS

Milwaukee Bucks won one of history's most important coin tosses to earn first pick in the 1970 NBA draft to sign Abdul-Jabbar (then Alcindor)

Abdul-Jabbar was known as Lew Alcindor during his record-breaking college career

## "ABDUL-JABBAR WAS A TRAILBLAZER IN HIS SHOT-MAKING, AN INSPIRATION, A MULTIPLE CHAMPION, A RECORD MACHINE WITH STATS UNLIKELY TO BE BROKEN"

Abdul-Jabbar was comfortably into his thirties during his Lakers glory years, but continued to dominate the stats tables, showing phenomenal levels of fitness for a man of his age. He credits yoga for his longevity but also there was an insatiable appetite for work and further success for himself and his team – younger colleagues were regularly bested and amazed by the effort he put into training and game day.

This drive and determination to succeed reached its pinnacle in 1984 when his signature skyhook landed during a game between the Lakers and Utah Jazz. The score moved Abdul-Jabbar onto 31,420 career NBA points – one ahead of Wilt Chamberlain's all-time record. Abdul-Jabbar would go on to score nearly 7,000 more points over the course of his career and – as of the start of the 2019–20 season – he is still nearly 1,500 points clear of his nearest challenger. And if you want to put that total down to sheer number of games played then that's doing a disservice to his field goal percentage of 55.9% – which is second only to Shaquille O'Neal among players to have scored over 20,000 NBA points. He possibly could have scored even more points were it not for his voracious love of defending his own basket. Only two men have made more blocks than Abdul-Jabbar, who proved his worth at both ends of the court.

1985 was the Lakers' fourth Finals in a row, and they won it, beating the Boston Celtics 4-2. Abdul-Jabbar top scored for the Lakers earning him a second Finals MVP award – 14 years after his first.

Abdul-Jabbar was 41 when he took to the court for the deciding game of the 1987–88 NBA season – with the reigning champions Lakers and Detroit Pistons locked at 3-3. Abdul-Jabbar started the game and although he scored just four points

Abdul-Jabbar has always stood by his beliefs – here he and the Celtics' Bill Russell (left) support Muhammad Ali following his refusal to be drafted for the Vietnam War

he made the only block by a Lakers player, which helped his side run out 108-105 winners. It was his sixth NBA championship title, and was to prove his last. One more season and one more Finals appearance followed, but this time the Pistons got their own back and routed the Lakers 4-0. At 42, Abdul-Jabbar had finally run out of steam and hung up his sneakers – bowing out of a game he had dominated for the past two decades. At the time of his retirement he held multiple records, including most MVP awards, most points, most blocks, most seasons played and most games played. A few of those records still stand today, over 30 years later, including those all-important points-scoring and MVP awards. Greats come and go – but it seems no one is getting close to challenging the supremacy of the legendary Kareem Abdul-Jabbar when it comes to the numbers.

He was inducted into the NBA Hall of Fame in 1995, just six years after his retirement, as well as being named in the NBA's 35th Anniversary Team and 50 Greatest Players in NBA History. However, it was to take some time before Abdul-Jabbar gained recognition from the team that he had brought so much silverware. Although his number 33 jersey was retired instantly upon his retirement, it wasn't until November 2012 that the Lakers unveiled a statue of their former center. Already in place at the Staples Center was a statue of Magic Johnson, as well as Jerry West, Lakers announcer Chick Hearn, and LA Kings star Wayne Gretsky. Abdul-Jabbar himself said that he thought the wait was something of a slight on him, something many fans agreed with.

Kareem Abdul-Jabbar was never one for the limelight despite his immense stature, both physically and professionally, repeatedly thrusting him into it. That may be one of the reasons he isn't held in quite as high esteem as many of his illustrious colleagues who don't have the awards, numbers or titles to come close to competing with him. He was a trailblazer in his shot-making, an inspiration due to his work ethic at both ends of the court, a multiple champion, a record machine with stats unlikely to be broken and an activist who stood by his beliefs no matter what the challenges. But, possibly above all, he was a humble, wise icon of the game whose poise, dignity and talent transcended the sport of basketball. And isn't that what a true legend should be?

## ROGER, ROGER

### KAREEM ABDUL-JABBAR'S TALENTS WEREN'T CONFINED TO THE BASKETBALL COURT, AS HIS LITERARY AND ACTING RECORDS SHOW

Kareem Abdul-Jabbar might not have been on the front pages as much as the back pages, but his post-basketball career saw him change all that and become a huge presence on television and in print.

He has written numerous books since his retirement, and not just the standard autobiography that so many churn out. He has co-authored over a dozen works, ranging from explorations of race and the Civil Rights Movement, to a fiction series about a young, gifted basketball player and even a series of comics focusing on the life of Mycroft Holmes – brother of the world-renowned Sherlock. He is also a four-time Southern California Journalism Awards Columnist of the Year winner, as well as a fixture on the punditry circuit, delivering his expertise to a generation that never got the chance to see him play.

Abdul-Jabbar was also a pioneer in Hollywood. Probably the first basketball player people think of when it comes to movies is Michael Jordan, thanks to his appearance in the 1996 movie *Space Jam*, but Abdul-Jabbar was doing it a decade earlier, with a role in the comedy-disaster movie *Airplane!*, as well as a number of guest appearances on TV shows. Truly a man of many talents.

Kareem Abdul-Jabbar's big screen appearance as Roger Murdock paved the way for the likes of Michael Jordan to earn Hollywood success

# NBA LEGENDS

# 10 GREATEST NBA GAMES OF ALL TIME

## THE MOMENTS THAT MADE THE NBA'S LEGACY – THE MOST EXTRAORDINARY, MOMENTOUS AND EXCITING GAMES IN THE LEAGUE'S RICH HISTORY

The history of NBA basketball is littered with momentous milestones, epic rivalries and unforgettable games throughout its 70-plus years. Choosing only ten games that stand out is a near-impossible task, but the ones we've chosen are all special in some way, whether it's the culmination of a rivalry, the moment a player becomes a superstar, the end of an era for a player or team, or a record-breaking game in some way or another. We tend to overvalue the recent and devalue the past, so we've included games from most eras. Most of them happen to involve a seminal superstar in NBA league history in an important role.

Finals games make several appearances, because when the pressure is most intense, the real heroes are revealed. So let's roll on to nine fantastic games in the NBA's history – and one that will forever live in infamy…

# 10 GREATEST NBA GAMES OF ALL TIME

## CONTROVERSY AND TEST OF ENDURANCE

**01** The 1976 regular season had been dominated by the Boston Celtics in the East and reigning champions Golden State Warriors in the West.

The Celtics won the title in 1974 and were laser-focused on reclaiming the trophy from the Warriors. They breezed through the playoffs, beating both the Braves and Cavs in six games, but their Finals opponent would surprise them.

The Phoenix Suns were a much younger team than the Celtics. They only just squeaked past the .500 mark in the regular season with 42 wins, but showed remarkable steel in the playoffs. The Suns and Celtics split the first four games, each winning two games at home, the last of which went to overtime before falling to the Suns by two points. The fifth game, however, would dwarf the combined drama of the series so far. As the game wound down, the teams were locked in battle with standout performances on both sides. The game went to triple overtime, with both teams finding themselves trying to call timeouts they didn't have. A court invasion by fans at the end of the first OT resulted in two seconds controversially added to the clock.

The Celtics finally eked out a win in the third OT, scoring 16 points to the Suns' 14 in those deciding five minutes. The Suns' Gar Heard played an unbelievable 61 minutes in the game, while the Celtics' White logged 60 of his own, scoring 33 points and tallying nine assists. This game wound up having a bigger effect on the young Suns who ran out of fuel in the sixth game, handing the Celtics the 1976 title.

**SCORE:** Phoenix Suns 126 – 128 Boston Celtics
**GAME:** NBA Finals Game 5
**DATE:** 4 June 1976
**VENUE:** Boston Garden, Boston

# NBA LEGENDS

Michael Jordan hitting the title-winning shot in the 1998 NBA Finals, his last-ever shot for the Bulls

## NBA'S HIGHEST-SCORING GAME EVER

**SCORE:** Denver Nuggets 184 – 186 Detroit Pistons
**GAME:** Regular Season Game 23
**DATE:** 13 December 1983
**VENUE:** McNichols Arena, Denver

**03** Today's NBA might be a high-scoring league, but it's got nothing on the 1980s. The four highest-scoring games in history all took place between 1982 and 1990, three of which the high-powered Denver Nuggets hosted.

In December 1983, the Nuggets and Detroit Pistons combined for a frankly dizzying 370 points in a triple-overtime game that broke several other records beside the scoring. Combined together, the team scored 142 field goals (but incredibly only two three-pointers), as well as 93 assists, while four players scored at least 40 points, led by Kiki VanDeWeghe's career-high 51 for Denver, who lost after 63 minutes of a historic offensive display by both teams.

Alex English scored 47 points for the Denver Nuggets, while Isiah Thomas equalled that number for Detroit and racked up 17 assists to boot, and John Long scored 41. Unsurprisingly, no defensive records were broken that night in Denver.

## THE FINAL MOMENT OF THE BULLS DYNASTY

**02** The 1997-98 Chicago Bulls had to work harder than they had in their two previous title-winning years. The entire core of their team was 29 or older, with Michael Jordan at 34 and heavily hinting at retirement at the end of the season.

The Jazz gave them all sorts of trouble in the Finals, where Karl Malone and John Stockton finally eyed an opportunity to step out from under the gigantic shadow Jordan and his running mate Scottie Pippen had cast on the league throughout the 1990s. Jordan cut the Jazz's lead to one point on a lay-up with 40 seconds to go. Chicago got a quick steal and Jordan dribbled down most of the clock before rising up for a flawless 20-footer over Byron Russell to clinch the Bulls' second three-peat of the decade. Jordan retired after the game – the perfect note for an all-time great (before he came back in 2001, of course).

**SCORE:** Chicago Bulls 87 – 86 Utah Jazz
**GAME:** NBA Finals Game 6
**DATE:** 14 June 1998
**VENUE:** Delta Center, Salt Lake City

Kiki VanDeWeghe, pictured here in 1982, scored a career high 51 points but still ended on the losing side

# 10 GREATEST NBA GAMES OF ALL TIME

## THE MALICE IN THE PALACE

Ron Artest being escorted off the floor after the worst brawl in NBA history, which resulted in a 73-game suspension for Artest

**04** Most of the games on this list earned their spot due to a historic achievement of some sort. The first regular-season matchup between Central Division rivals Indiana and Detroit in the 2004-05 season did not.

Instead, this fairly unexciting game, taking place on a chilly November evening will forever live in infamy for the violent brawl that unfolded with 45.9 seconds remaining in the fourth quarter. After the Pacers' Ron Artest (now Metta World Peace) hit Detroit center Ben Wallace in the back of the head as the latter went up for a lay-up, Wallace retaliated by pushing Artest in the face. After a fist fight between several players from both teams, things seemed to be settling down, until Artest was hit by a flying drink cup from the stands. He leapt into the stands, punched a fan (who happened to be a different man to the one who had thrown the cup), and all hell promptly broke loose. Fans invaded the court, attacking players, some of whom responded with full-blown counterpunches. Meanwhile, other players ended up in scuffles in the stands, while coaches, referees and yet more players tried to either escape the arena or break up fights between teammates and fans. The game was called off and the final 45 seconds were never played.

Several players received hefty suspensions and fines, Artest the longest one as he was suspended for the remainder of the season, missing 73 regular season and 13 playoff games and forfeiting almost $5 million in salaries. Several players and fans also received criminal sentences as a result of the 'Malice In The Palace'.

**SCORE:** Indiana Pacers 97 – 82 Detroit Pistons
**GAME:** Regular Season Game 8
**DATE:** 19 November 2004
**VENUE:** The Palace of Auburn Hills, Michigan

## SIMPLY MAGIC

**05** The Lakers-Sixers NBA Finals series of 1980 was a delicately balanced one, with no team ever winning by more than ten points in the first five games.

The difference maker for most of the series was the Lakers' unstoppable center, Kareem Abdul-Jabbar, who averaged an incredible 33.4 points per game in the first five games, propelling the Lakers to a 3-2 series lead over Julius Erving and his Sixers squad.

But Abdul-Jabbar twisted his ankle badly in the third quarter of Game 5, and although he managed to finish the game, he was eventually ruled out of Game 6. In an inspired move, coach Paul Westhead moved rookie point guard Magic Johnson into the center role. The 6' 9" phenomenon had no problem adjusting and racked up 42 points, 15 rebounds, seven assists, three steals and a block in one of the most dominant Finals displays in history. He was unsurprisingly named Finals MVP and instantly became a superstar.

**SCORE:** Los Angeles Lakers 123 – 107 Philadelphia 76ers
**GAME:** NBA Finals Game 6
**DATE:** 16 May 1980
**VENUE:** The Spectrum, Philadelphia

Magic Johnson was extremely tall for a point guard, which gave the Lakers a surprising trump card when Kareem Abdul-Jabbar got injured

# NBA LEGENDS

*Jordan celebrates scoring the series-winning shot against the Cavs*

## THE SHOT™

**06** The lasting memory of what's perhaps Michael Jordan's most iconic moment is his jumping celebration after hitting the series-winning shot over Craig Ehlo and the Cavs in the first round of the 1989 playoffs.

However, that wild display of emotion wasn't broadcast live at the time, as the live cameras were focused on Bulls coach Doug Collins' sprint down the sideline to his team. And while Jordan's unforgettable dagger is indeed iconic, it was only the final exclamation mark to an epic game that was closely fought throughout.

Having won all six regular season meetings between the teams, the Cavs' strength in depth had them pegged as the favourites in their playoffs series. Despite 50 points from Michael Jordan in Game 4, the Cavs won and forced a decider on their home court, but Ron Harper and Craig Ehlo, who took turns defending Jordan, could do nothing to stop a third-straight 40-plus performance from him, including the dramatic final shot from the foul circle that added the first of what would be many feathers to Jordan's playoff hat, and one of many, many agonising memories for Cleveland fans.

**SCORE:** Chicago Bulls 101 – 100 Cleveland Cavaliers
**GAME:** Eastern Conference First Round Game 5
**DATE:** 7 May 1989
**VENUE:** Coliseum at Richfield, Ohio

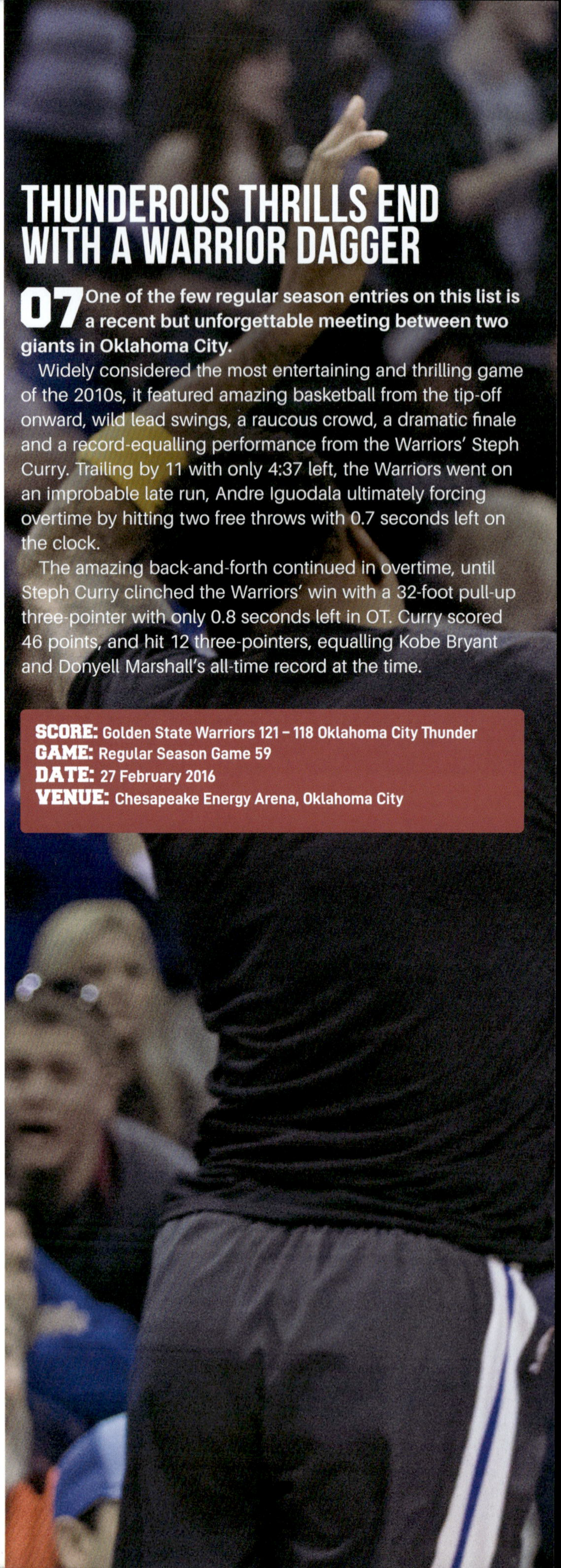

## THUNDEROUS THRILLS END WITH A WARRIOR DAGGER

**07** One of the few regular season entries on this list is a recent but unforgettable meeting between two giants in Oklahoma City.

Widely considered the most entertaining and thrilling game of the 2010s, it featured amazing basketball from the tip-off onward, wild lead swings, a raucous crowd, a dramatic finale and a record-equalling performance from the Warriors' Steph Curry. Trailing by 11 with only 4:37 left, the Warriors went on an improbable late run, Andre Iguodala ultimately forcing overtime by hitting two free throws with 0.7 seconds left on the clock.

The amazing back-and-forth continued in overtime, until Steph Curry clinched the Warriors' win with a 32-foot pull-up three-pointer with only 0.8 seconds left in OT. Curry scored 46 points, and hit 12 three-pointers, equalling Kobe Bryant and Donyell Marshall's all-time record at the time.

**SCORE:** Golden State Warriors 121 – 118 Oklahoma City Thunder
**GAME:** Regular Season Game 59
**DATE:** 27 February 2016
**VENUE:** Chesapeake Energy Arena, Oklahoma City

# NBA LEGENDS

## 25 IN A ROW FOR LEBRON

**08** LeBron James put on a performance for the ages in the epic final quarter of Game 5 against the Pistons in the Eastern Conference Finals. The team-focused Pistons had ground the Cavs' offense to a halt in the first two games of the matchup before the Cavs fought back in games 3 and 4.

However, the Detroit Pistons seemed equal to the task in a closely fought fifth game at home until James took over late in the fourth in one of the greatest playoff performances in history. He scored the Cavaliers' last seven points in the fourth, including the game-tying lay-up to send it to overtime, and then proceeded to score every single one of their 18 points in the two overtime periods, ultimately dragging the Cleveland Cavaliers to a win, and a series lead they would not relinquish. He finished the game with an impressive 48 points.

**SCORE:** Cleveland Cavaliers 109 – 107 Detroit Pistons
**GAME:** Eastern Conference Finals Game 5
**DATE:** 31 May 2007
**VENUE:** The Palace of Auburn Hills, Michigan

LeBron James scored the Cavaliers' final 25 points of the game to secure the win

John Paxson, seen here in Game 5, hit a decisive three-pointer to secure victory and the Bull's first three-peat

## BULLS CLINCH THEIR FIRST THREE-PEAT

**09** The Chicago Bulls came into the 1992-93 season as back-to-back champions, but the Phoenix Suns had designs on preventing a historic three-peat.

They had acquired Charles Barkley in the offseason in an attempt to get the first title in both Barkley's career and the Suns' history. And they came oh so close to achieving the aims. Despite dropping the first two games of the Finals at home, Phoenix fought back to force a sixth game and the chance to get a decider at home.

And the Suns led 98-94 after a strong fourth quarter with the clock running down. Michael Jordan cut the lead to two with a lay-up, and after a missed three-pointer from Dan Majerle, the Bulls got their chance. The hero, however, would be an unexpected one. As Suns player Danny Ainge left back-up shooter John Paxson free to double-team Horace Grant, who was not a great offensive player, Grant passed out to Paxson, who easily sank the decisive three-pointer with 3.9 seconds to spare. Paxson's heroics were then followed up by a last-second block from Grant on Kevin Johnson to clinch the Bulls' first three-peat in dramatic fashion.

**SCORE:** Chicago Bulls 99 – 98 Phoenix Suns
**GAME:** NBA Finals Game 6
**DATE:** 20 June 1993
**VENUE:** America West Arena, Phoenix

# 10 GREATEST NBA GAMES OF ALL TIME

Larry Bird scored 29 points and grabbed 21 rebounds as the Celtics took charge of the series

## THE GREATEST FINALS GAME EVER?

**10** The 1980s were largely defined by two teams – and their charismatic leaders; Larry Bird's Boston Celtics and Magic Johnson's Los Angeles Lakers.

The two teams – and players – went about their success in wildly different fashion, however. While the 'Showtime' Lakers lit up the league with their flashy, fast-paced basketball, the Celtics took on a more hard-nosed identity.

In 1984 it seemed the Lakers would finally get the better of their rivals, blowing out the Celtics in Game 3, 137-104, behind a Finals record 21 assists from Magic Johnson. Larry Bird ripped into his own team after that game, calling them sissies and publicly urging them to toughen up. And toughen up they did.

Game 4 would turn out to be a matchup for the ages. The Lakers took a ten-point lead into half-time but the Celtics gradually cut into it as the game wore on. The Lakers led by five with under a minute left, but an uncharacteristic bad pass by Magic, intercepted by Parish, helped the Celtics even up the score and force overtime. The Celtics pulled away in OT, ultimately winning by four and tying up the series. Magic tallied a triple-double with 20 points, 11 rebounds and 17 assists, but it wasn't enough to counter Bird's monster game of 29 points and 21 rebounds.

The Celtics managed to rattle the Lakers because they were ultra-physical throughout. That night, Bird solidified himself as a bona-fide NBA superstar, and perhaps one of the most ruthlessly competitive players in the league's history.

**SCORE:** Boston Celtics 129 – 125 Los Angeles Lakers
**GAME:** NBA Finals Game 4
**DATE:** 6 June 1984
**VENUE:** The Forum, Inglewood

# EARVIN 'MAGIC' JOHNSON

**POSITION:** Point Guard
**NBA DRAFT:** 1979/Round 1/Pick 1
**CAREER:** LA Lakers (1979-1991, 1996)

**HIGHLIGHTS:**
5x NBA Champion (1980, 1982, 1985, 1987, 1988)
3x NBA MVP (1987, 1989, 1990)
3x NBA Finals MVP (1980, 1982, 1987)
12x NBA All-Star Team (1980, 1982-1992)
10x All-NBA Team (1982-1991)
4x assists leader (1983, 1984, 1986, 1987)
2x steals leader (1981, 1982)

**STATS:**
**REGULAR SEASON**
Points: 17,707 | Assists: 10,141 | Steals: 1,724

**PLAYOFFS**
Points: 3,701 | Assists: 2,346 | Steals: 358

Magic Johnson became a media darling not least due to his infectious smile and outgoing personality

# THE SHOWTIME MAGICIAN

## BREATHING NEW LIFE INTO THE NBA ON HIS ARRIVAL, MAGIC JOHNSON'S LARGER-THAN-LIFE PERSONA AND PLAYING STYLE DEFINED THE 1980S' LAKERS DYNASTY

Magic led the Lakers to two Finals victories over arch rivals the Boston Celtics in 1985 and 1987

In his rookie season, Magic Johnson started at center in Game 6 of the Finals against the 76ers, scoring 42 points and winning the championship in the process

A lot of players have changed the face of the NBA at one time or another. But if it hadn't been for Magic Johnson, the league might not even exist at all today. In the 1970s, the NBA was far from the money-making juggernaut it is today. After a costly battle for players, spectators and TV coverage between the ABA and NBA during the early 1970s, when both leagues haemorrhaged money every year, the ABA finally folded in 1976.

Four of the best ABA teams were adopted by the NBA in an effort to expand the league and make it viable, but without a dominant franchise, lucrative TV contracts and dwindling spectator numbers, the NBA still found itself in a precarious position as the 1980s approached. But it found salvation in two larger-than-life personalities who would come to shape the next decade of basketball and reignite the league's most prestigious rivalry in the process. The first was the Boston Celtics' Larry Bird, a hard-nosed, ultra-competitive forward who oozed both skill and self-confidence to match. The other was Earvin 'Magic' Johnson. Magic was drafted first overall in 1979, joining a resurgent Lakers team under new ownership, after Jerry Buss had bought the franchise earlier that year. He aimed to return the Lakers to contention, by quickly rebuilding the team around superstar Kareem Abdul-Jabbar and reigniting a sense of excitement around it. And Magic's arrival in the draft made an immediate impact. Resuming his personal rivalry with the Celtics' Bird, who he had faced several times in college, Johnson provided an all-around threat as a playmaking guard for the Lakers.

At 6-feet 9-inches, he was extremely tall for his position, usually reserved for players under 6-feet 6-inches. He had unparalleled court vision, was very cool under pressure

## "WHILE HIS MAIN FOCUS WAS ON THE OFFENSIVE END, HE COULD DEFEND ANY POSITION ON THE FLOOR, FROM POINT GUARD TO CENTER"

and, while his main focus was on the offensive end, he could defend any position on the floor, from point guard to center, closing down passing lanes with ease. The Lakers became an immediate frontrunner in the Western Conference, setting up an eventual run all the way to the Finals. This was a godsend for the struggling NBA; two young, charismatic stars with a personal sporting rivalry already established in college, each leading one of the league's most storied franchises to the NBA Finals in their first season.

TV networks were interested in the league again, basketball made it back to the front pages of the newspapers' sports sections, and even opposing teams' fans turned out in numbers to watch Magic when he came.

But in Los Angeles, Magic was doing more than just playing well; he was reshaping the way basketball was played. After a decade of perhaps less than glamorous basketball, where tough-nosed tactics reigned supreme, and workmanlike players such as Bill Walton and Wes Unseld were leading their teams to championships, Magic was a breath of fresh air. He possessed great technical ability, and even more so, a flair for the spectacular. He brought showmanship to the team from Hollywood, throwing no-look passes and highlight-worthy alley-oops to his teammates on a nightly basis, getting by defenders both with inventive moves, ball-handling skills and magician-like misdirection. The new Lakers, led by Magic, were more than a sports team, they were entertainment. The term 'Showtime' was soon affixed to them, and it soon attracted a high-profile

Magic led the run-and-gun-style 'Showtime Lakers' with his quick passing and incisive attacking style

# EARVIN 'MAGIC' JOHNSON

## BEST OF RIVALS

**MAGIC JOHNSON AND LARRY BIRD'S NBA JOURNEY SHARED HIGHS, LOWS AND A CAREER-LONG RIVALRY, AS WELL AS A DEEP BOND**

It's almost impossible to talk about Magic Johnson and his impact on the NBA without mentioning Larry Bird in the same breath.

Their paths first crossed in college, in one of the most-watched NCAA championship games ever, when Magic's Michigan State beat Bird's then-undefeated Indiana State 75-64. They joined the NBA the same year, and through it reignited the classic Celtics-Lakers rivalry that had dominated the NBA in the 1960s.

In 1984, the Celtics and Lakers met in the Finals again, for the first of three times that decade. After Bird drew first blood that year, Magic would win the next two matchups, in 1985 and 1987.

But despite that fierce sporting rivalry, which often became very physical on the court, the two became good friends off it, sharing their underprivileged Midwestern roots and intense passion for the game.

When Magic was diagnosed with HIV in 1991, Bird was one of the first people he called, and when Bird retired the following year due to injury, Magic joined him at his jersey-retirement ceremony in Boston. And in 1992, they finally got to play together when they were both selected to the men's US basketball team for the Olympics where the 'Dream Team' bulldozed its way to a dominant gold medal. It was the perfect bookend to the greatest rivalry in NBA history.

celebrity following. But if Magic's eye-opening rookie season, where he averaged 18 points, 7.7 rebounds, 7.3 assists and 2.4 steals per game, made him a star, the 1980 Finals established his status as a sporting icon and superstar.

In a hard-fought best-of-seven series against the Philadelphia 76ers, which was led by Darryl Dawkins, Maurice Cheeks and high-flying, ex-ABA superstar Julius Erving, the Lakers took a 3-2 lead behind immense production from Kareem Abdul-Jabbar, who was averaging 33.4 points, 13.6 rebounds and 4.6 blocks per game. No game had been decided by more than ten points, and seemed destined to go to a deciding Game 7, as midway through Game 5, Abdul-Jabbar injured his ankle. Despite returning to the last quarter in that game, he was soon ruled out for the next game, leaving the Lakers short-handed at the center position, for the vital matchup against Dawkins. Instead of promoting backup center Mark Landsberger to the starting lineup for Game 6, however, coach Paul Westhead made the bold move to start Magic at center. The result? Magic had a monster of a game, with 42 points, 15 rebounds and seven assists, leading the Showtime Lakers to a 123-107 win and the team's first championship since 1972. Magic was crowned Finals MVP.

The 1980s would come to be dominated by Magic's highly entertaining Lakers. Only twice did they fail to make the Finals between 1980 and 1989, and both times they were stopped by the same team; the Houston Rockets. The first time was in 1981, when the sixth-seeded Rockets caused a shock upset in the first round of the playoffs. They beat the Lakers 2-1 in a best-of-three series, led by a mammoth performance by center Moses Malone, while Magic struggled, shooting only 39% from the field and 65% from the free-throw line after an injury-riddled season. In response,

Larry Bird and Magic Johnson's rivalry forged a bond that extended far beyond the basketball court

# NBA LEGENDS

## LIFE AFTER SHOWTIME

### MAGIC FACED – AND OVERCAME – HIS BIGGEST CHALLENGES AFTER HIS PLAYING CAREER FINISHED

Magic Johnson was only 31 years old and still among the best players in the NBA when his playing career was abruptly cut short by his HIV diagnosis.

At that time, stigma and prejudice regarding HIV was still rampant, with many seeing an HIV diagnosis effectively as a death sentence. However, Magic Johnson tirelessly worked on changing that perception, for example by showing you can still lead a healthy, active life, by winning the All-Star MVP award at the 1992 All-Star Game, and by reducing people's fear of being around HIV-positive people as well as using his outgoing personality and honesty about his past and what led to him contracting the virus to help people avoid getting HIV in the first place.

His immense fame also highlighted the work being done to find a treatment to minimise the effects and risks of HIV, which has developed by leaps and bounds in the last few decades, making that treatment available to everyone who needs it, and hopefully one day find a cure. He has also become involved in the NBA as an ambassador for the sport, and recently as an executive, serving as president of basketball operations from 2017 to 2019.

Magic used his physical strength to his advantage as a tall point guard who could rebound, pass and score

Magic Johnson, here at the 2018 Draft Combine, has stayed deeply involved with basketball since retirement

Pat Riley replaced Westhead as head coach, and under his leadership, Magic became a near-unstoppable force for years to come. In the first two rounds of the 1982 playoffs, Magic averaged a triple-double as the Lakers swept their way to the Finals, where they again encountered the trio of Erving, Cheeks and Dawkins and the 76ers, now reinforced by high-scoring shooting guard Andrew Toney. However, the more balanced Lakers team again won in six games, and again Magic won the Finals MVP award.

In 1983, the 76ers awaited the Lakers again, now new and improved with Moses Malone aboard. With the Lakers' star center, Abdul-Jabbar, now 35 years old, Malone dominated the series on the way to a 4-0 Sixers sweep. In 1984, however, the Lakers would finally face the old nemesis, the Celtics, in the Finals. After beating the Kings, Mavericks and Suns on the way to the Finals, Magic and Bird finally met in the Finals. It was a dream come true for all avid basketball fans, and the two fierce competitors and ex-college rivals didn't disappoint.

Magic and Bird led their teams through an epic series that went all the way to a Game 7, where Bird's incredible scoring skills were matched each step of the way by Magic's talent as a facilitator. However, in the deciding game, Bird and his hard-nosed Celtics managed to grind through the Los Angeles' flashy squad.

Magic would need more support to regain the title for his Showtime Lakers. While still a 20-plus scorer, Abdul-Jabbar was entering the twilight of his career, so others would need to step up. Thankfully, that support emerged from within, as athletic young co-stars James Worthy and Byron Scott quickly blossomed into more than capable running mates for Magic's fast and furious playing style. The 1985 Finals provided a grudge match with the Celtics, and this time the Lakers prevailed in six games, with Magic dishing out a frankly absurd 14 assists per game in the series and 15.2 on average throughout the playoffs.

1986 was the only other hiccup in the Lakers and Magic's otherwise unbroken reign as overlords of the Western Conference between 1982 and 1989, and like in 1981, their march was stopped by the Houston Rockets. This 1986 Rockets team was a particularly tricky matchup for the run-and-gun Lakers, led by the 'Two Towers', two supremely talented centers in the 7-foot four-inch Ralph Sampson and 7-foot-tall Hakeem Olajuwon. Despite Magic averaging an unreal 16.2 assists per game against the Rockets, Houston prevailed in five games before falling to the Celtics in the Finals.

# EARVIN 'MAGIC' JOHNSON

> "FAR FROM LYING DOWN AND GIVING UP, THOUGH, MAGIC TOOK THIS DEFEAT AS A MESSAGE TO GET EVEN MORE ASSERTIVE ON OFFENSE"

Far from lying down and giving up, though, Magic took this defeat as a message to get even more assertive on offense, and the following season, he averaged a career-high 23.9 points per game, after having hovered around the 18-point average for most of his first seven seasons in the league. He also averaged 12.2 assists per game that season, leading the league in assists for the fourth time in his career, and in return he won his first regular season MVP award, enjoyed another trip to the NBA Finals, another matchup against the Celtics, another win in six games against his archrival, and a third Finals MVP award to boot.

1988 saw the Lakers repeat as champions, and although Magic ceded the Finals MVP trophy to teammate James Worthy that year, he still showed out with 21.1 points and 13 assists per game in a hard-fought seven-game series against the physical Detroit Pistons, on top of a regular-season showing where he came third in MVP voting after averaging 19.6 points and 11.9 assists per game.

However, time was finally catching up with the Showtime Lakers. The 41-year-old Kareem Abdul-Jabbar was close to retirement, and even though new supporting players AC Green and veteran Mychal Thompson were more than capable players, the team couldn't retain the title come spring 1989. Despite another MVP season by Magic, the Pistons tore through the Lakers in only four games, led by Joe Dumars' hot shooting and Isiah Thomas's slick playmaking.

Magic completed the MVP trifecta in 1990, after averaging over 22 points for the second season in a row, but that year the top-seeded Lakers suffered a shock 4-1 defeat to fifth seeds Phoenix Suns in the semifinals of the playoffs. It mattered little that Magic averaged over 30 points per game in the series, as opposing star point guard Kevin Johnson had his way on offense with 22 points and 11.2 assists per game.

But with a retooled roster, having signed Sam Perkins as a free agent in the summer of 1990 and promoted second-year center Vlade Divac to the starting lineup, the Lakers found their way to the Finals for an astonishing ninth time in Magic Johnson's 12 years with the team. However, the Lakers came up just short again, this time against the new king of the NBA, Michael Jordan and his Chicago Bulls. Despite two triple-doubles from Magic in the series, the Bulls defeated the Lakers in five games on their way to the first title in their franchise history.

But this on-court defeat paled in comparison to the shock to come off the court later in 1991. On the eve of the 1991–92 season, Magic tested positive for HIV during a physical exam. After being absent for the Lakers' first three games, Magic publicly announced

Magic pours a bottle of champagne over Lakers owner Jerry Buss after winning the 1980 NBA Finals

the diagnosis on 7 November. He also announced his immediate retirement at the same time, to focus on fighting the disease. He quickly became a vocal leader in the fight for public awareness of HIV, against the stigma it bore at that time and to help people become informed about the disease and learn how to avoid contracting it.

But despite being retired, he was voted in by fans as a starter for the 1992 All-Star Game, and although some players voiced concerns about the risk of him playing, he not only showed up, but led the West to a thumping victory over the East and won himself the All-Star Game MVP award in the process.

Further glory followed that summer, as Magic was chosen to represent the USA National Basketball Team for the 1992 Olympics, the first Olympic Games where professional basketball players were allowed to compete for their countries. He appeared in six out of the team's eight games on the USA's way to an utterly dominant Olympic title, averaging 8.0 points and 5.5 assists per game, and repeatedly earning standing ovations from fans.

His playing career saw one final entry, over three years later. After four seasons out of the NBA, Magic rejoined the Lakers, and despite being a little heavier, a little older and a little slower, he helped the team reach the fourth seed in the Western Conference with 14.6 points, 5.7 rebounds and 6.9 assists in 32 games, but his comeback concluded with a first-round finish in the playoffs, and somewhat fittingly, just like a decade earlier, the exit came against Hakeem Olajuwon's Houston Rockets.

## NBA LEGENDS

### LEBRON JAMES

**POSITION:** Power Forward, Small Forward
**NBA DRAFT:** 2003/Round 1/Pick 1
**CAREER:** Cleveland Cavaliers (2003-2010, 2014-2018), Miami Heat (2010-2014), LA Lakers (2018-present)

#### HIGHLIGHTS:
3x NBA Champion (2012, 2013, 2016)
4x NBA MVP (2009, 2010, 2012, 2013)
3x NBA Finals MVP (2012, 2013, 2016)
16x NBA All-Star Team (2005-20)
15x All-NBA Team (2005-19)
5x NBA All-Defensive First Team (2009-13)
1x NBA Rookie of the Year (2004)
1x NBA scoring champion (2008)

#### STATS:
**REGULAR SEASON**
Points: 33,918 | Assists: 9,235 | Rebounds: 9,298

**PLAYOFFS**
Points: 6,911 | Assists: 1,687 | Rebounds: 2,122

James dunks against the Golden State Warriors in 2017

# IN THE COURT OF KING JAMES

## VERY FEW PLAYERS HAVE GONE FROM 'PREP-TO-PRO', BUT VERY FEW HAVE THE TALENT OF LEBRON JAMES

Few events in professional sport can match the frenzied reaction to LeBron James's decision on 8 July 2010 to leave his hometown Cavaliers and join the Miami Heat as a free agent. The sports world imploded.

Free agents have moved from one team to another in all major sports. Sometimes the moves attract criticism; sometimes they pass by relatively unnoticed. In James's case, he instantly went from one of the most popular NBA stars to a man reviled as much as legendary traitor Benedict Arnold, who plotted to sell out an American fort to the British during the American War of Independence. At first glance, moving from one NBA team to another was not in the same league as Arnold's treachery, but there were reasons behind the uproar.

First of all, James had failed to deliver on his promise to bring a championship to Cleveland. After joining the Cavaliers in 2003 as a 'prep-to-pro' phenomenon (meaning that he skipped college and jumped to the NBA straight out of high school), he had been viewed as a saviour and had indeed transformed the fortunes of the franchise. From a sorry 17-65 in the season before he arrived, James lifted Cleveland into the playoffs in 2006 and into the NBA Finals in 2007. But the Cavaliers had been whitewashed by the San Antonio Spurs in that series and had not returned to the Finals in the years since.

Cleveland fans felt betrayed by James's decision to leave them in the lurch, and the manner in which his decision was announced struck many observers as offensive. While most big-name free agents satisfy themselves with a press conference, James was the subject of a live TV special. It was a shocking fall from grace for one of the most high-profile athletes in global sport, and it would take James years to rebuild his reputation.

James was special from the start. Few players have bypassed college and joined the NBA straight out of high school. Most of those that did took time to adjust, and even legends like Kobe Bryant and Kevin Garnett experienced their struggles.

# NBA LEGENDS

King James brings a title to Cleveland in 2016

James won his first championship against Oklahoma City in the 2012 NBA Finals

Many people expected James to struggle as well, but there were also reasons to suspect he might transition more smoothly to the pro game. James was a big man in high school, standing at 6-feet 8-inches and weighing around 240 pounds. He had the physique to match the NBA's big men while not long being out of childhood at the age of 18.

That physique had served him well at Saint Vincent-Saint Mary High School. Along with his good friends (Sian Cotton, Dru Joyce III and Willie McGee), James was part of the legendary 'Fab Four' (they would become the 'Fab Five' with the addition of Romeo Travis). The high-school stars featured in the 2008 documentary *More than a Game*, but James was already a legendary player by that time.

With St Vincent-St Mary, James landed state titles in each of his first two seasons, before over-confidence cost the team a third straight. His final season appeared ruined when he was suspended for the year over an illegal car loan, but on appeal his suspension was reduced to just two games and he was able to help his school to its third title in four years.

James playing for Saint Vincent-Saint Mary. He became the first high-school player to make the cover of *Sports Illustrated*

Skipping college seemed the natural decision to make, but while nobody had any doubts over James's physical prowess, there were those who had concerns over his mental durability. The hype surrounding him would inevitably put a target on his back in the pros, and although he was well equipped to handle that physically, would his psyche survive being a marked man at such a young age?

James's decision to turn pro came at a good time for the NBA. A generation of legends was fading away and new names were needed to maintain the league's popularity. James chose to enter the league in the same draft as other big-time prospects, including Carmelo Anthony, Chris Bosh and Dwyane Wade. The draft lottery would determine where James ended up playing, as he was the clear choice to go with in the first pick.

With the lottery televised live, there was great excitement as one by one the teams were drawn. Toronto took the fourth pick, Denver the third and Memphis the second. The first pick then went to Cleveland, and James would be starting his professional career in his home state.

He wasn't exactly delighted. The franchise was on its knees and he had attended games, emerging unimpressed by the standard of play and the lack of fans at home games. On the other hand, it was an opportunity to make himself a living legend in a city starved of sporting success.

No pro sports team had won a championship for Cleveland since the Browns had landed the NFL title in 1964. There was

# LEBRON JAMES

a while it seemed like he would be able to get the job done himself. He was a starter in the All-Star Game, but the season was the opposite of his rookie campaign – the Cavaliers started strong but faded in the second half of the season, finishing at 42-40.

The next season, James took the Cavs over the hump, helping them to 50 wins and a place in the playoffs after a seven-year absence. A first-round playoff victory over the Washington Wizards served notice that the James-led Cavaliers were in business. James was in the conversation for the MVP award, having averaged 31.4 points per game, as well as making the All-NBA First Team.

In the 2006-07 campaign Cavaliers fans were delirious as their team made the NBA Finals, only to be swept by the San Antonio Spurs in a crushingly disappointing series.

Playoff appearances the next three seasons all saw the team progress at least past the first round. In 2008 James was part of the 'Redeem Team' that won Olympic gold in Beijing, but the Cavaliers were marking time and James would be a free agent in the 2010 offseason.

New players were brought in to strengthen the squad – the biggest name being a fading Shaquille O'Neal in 2009 – but the chances were James would be looking to move on in 2010.

James would be labelled many things after deciding to leave the Cavaliers in free agency. 'Traitor' and 'turncoat' were among

> "WHATEVER THE UNDERLYING REASONS BEHIND HIS MOVE, IT TURNED OUT TO BE AN INSPIRED DECISION. JAMES'S CAREER WAS ABOUT TO GO STRATOSPHERIC"

talk of a curse, and the city had been rocked by the decision of Art Modell to move the city's football team to Baltimore in 1995. If James could bring a title to Cleveland, he would become something close to a saint in the city.

Making a mockery of the doubters who had expected him to struggle, James transitioned to the pros quickly. The woes of the Cavaliers were too substantial to be overcome immediately, but by the second half of his first season, Cleveland was already a respectable team and James was on his way to Rookie of the Year honours.

In his second year, he became the youngest player ever to reach 2,000 career points, beating the mark set by Kobe Bryant by more than a year. On 19 January 2005, he turned in his first triple-double game, with 27 points, 11 rebounds and ten assists. Again, he was the youngest player ever to achieve the feat.

On 20 March of the same year he hit 56 points, but the Cavaliers still lost the game. James was having to carry the team until management could build it up around him, but for

## THE DECISION

### JAMES KEPT EVERYONE GUESSING ABOUT WHERE HE INTENDED TO PLAY IN 2010, INCLUDING THE CAVALIERS

LeBron James's initial departure from Cleveland could hardly have been handled more poorly. The live TV special, broadcast on ESPN, was widely viewed as little more than a vanity project. With a title of *The Decision*, the special dragged out for over an hour. To make matters worse, the Cavaliers were not informed of James's final choice until shortly before the programme aired.

After teasing his audience for half an hour before revealing that he was moving to Miami, most neutral fans were left questioning the decision to make the show, while Cavaliers fans vowed never to forgive him and sportswriters competed to condemn him in the harshest terms.

James's habit of referring to himself in the third person, endearing to Cleveland fans while he was 'one of them', now seemed arrogant and self-centred.

"I didn't want to make an emotional decision," James declared in the TV special. "I wanted to do what was best for LeBron James and what would make him happy. This is a business and I had seven great years in Cleveland. I hope the fans understand; maybe they won't."

# NBA LEGENDS

James goes up against Kobe during his first spell at the Cavaliers

James (left) with the other members of the original 'Fab Four'

the most painful insults, but 'mercenary' was also thrown around. This was unfair, as James could have earned more money if he'd stayed in Cleveland. The complicated NBA salary cap meant the Cavaliers could offer him a maximum contract, but he chose to play for less money with the Miami Heat.

What the Miami franchise could offer was a stronger supporting cast and the chance to win titles, and that was more important than money – not that James would exactly be playing for peanuts. "It is going to give me the best opportunity to win and win for multiple years," James said when talking about his decision. "I want to win championships and I feel like I can compete down there."

At the same time, James was far from oblivious to the distress he was causing in Cleveland, and the fact that he had failed to deliver the championship the city so desperately needed. "I feel awful that I'm leaving," he admitted. "I feel even worse that I wasn't able to bring an NBA championship to that city. To my real fans out there, I hope you continue to support me."

## "THERE WAS UNFINISHED BUSINESS IN CLEVELAND, AND KING JAMES WAS COMING HOME"

Whatever the underlying reasons behind his move, it turned out to be an inspired decision. James's career was about to go stratospheric. He would play in the next eight NBA Finals.

James had made efforts to recruit Chris Bosh to the Cavaliers, but the 6-foot 11-inch power forward chose Miami. Also moving to the Heat was Dwyane Wade, meaning that three of the top-five picks in the 2003 draft would suit up for Miami in the 2010–2011 season. It was a devastating combination, and although it took time for the new faces to gel, a players-only meeting helped change the Heat's trajectory. Winning 21 of its next 22 games, it was a force.

James was the pantomime villain of the league, heavily booed whenever the Heat travelled to play, and many quietly gloated when he suffered through a poor 2011 Finals, as the Heat lost in six games to Dallas.

The following season, however, Miami won the first of two consecutive titles. James won his third MVP award for the 2011–2012 season and in the Finals he clinched victory in Game 5 with a triple-double performance. James had proven the doubters wrong and he would never again have to listen to the whispers that he couldn't win the big games.

James switched from small forward to power forward the next year, as Bosh transitioned to center. James's game was maturing. His speed was an asset in his new position, but so was his new-found awareness of when to shoot. Better shot selection saw his percentage from the floor rise to 56.5. Now at his peak, he narrowly missed becoming the first ever unanimous MVP by a single vote. A 37-point effort in Game 7 of the Finals against the Spurs saw the Heat repeat.

LeBron dunks during the gold medal match at the 2012 London Olympics

# COMMITMENT TO EXCELLENCE
## LIKE MANY GREAT ATHLETES, JAMES HAS COUPLED NATURAL ABILITY WITH AN INSATIABLE APPETITE FOR HARD WORK

As is common with players with unusually long careers, James is dedicated to a punishing workout routine. As he moved into his thirties, he actually improved, where many other legends had seen their physical capabilities diminish with age.

James works out at least five times a week, adding in classes including Pilates. Although he could have easily taken things easy, he forces himself to get up at 5am and makes sure to play basketball every day to keep his skills honed.

Watching what he eats is another key element to his conditioning. The physical demands of being a professional basketball player demand a heavy calorific intake, but James chooses to fill that requirement with healthy foods: chicken, vegetables and pasta. Protein shakes supplement his diet and help prevent his body from breaking down.

The result is a frame capable of withstanding the extraordinary rigours of playing in eight consecutive Finals series and playing in at least 20 playoff games in seven out of eight years.

Another trip to the Finals (ending in defeat to the Spurs) saw James's Miami adventure come to an end. There was unfinished business in Cleveland, and King James was coming home.

"When I left Cleveland, I was on a mission," James explained in a *Sports Illustrated* feature after deciding to return to the Cavaliers for the 2014-2015 season. "I was seeking championships, and we won two. My goal is still to win as many titles as possible, no question. But what's most important for me is bringing one trophy back to Northeast Ohio."

James would finally deliver the longed-for title. The Cavaliers, in fact, made four consecutive Finals, and won the championship in 2016 when they beat the Warriors, rallying from a 1-3 deficit to win in seven games.

The milestones kept coming. He became the youngest player to reach 24,000 points (again beating Kobe Bryant by more than a year) and he passed Scottie Pippen to become the all-time leader in assists for a forward.

Never one to stay put for too long, however, James was on the move again in 2018, signing a four-year, $153.3 million contract with the Lakers. This time, although there was sadness that he was leaving, there was little of the bitterness that had marked his first departure from the Cavs. He was leaving the team as the leader in almost every statistical category that mattered, and he had delivered that one precious NBA title to a city that had been starved for success.

The move is just one more expression of James' desire to win and to make a difference to his team. "I believe the Lakers is a historical franchise," he said after announcing his latest move. "We all know that, but it's a championship franchise and that's what we're trying to get back to. I'm happy to be a part of the culture and be a part of us getting back to that point."

James left the Cavs for a second time in 2018, joining the LA Lakers

James warms up prior to a game with the LA Lakers

# THE ADMIRAL'S LONG MARCH

## DAVID ROBINSON TURNED THE FORTUNES OF AN AMBITIOUS FRANCHISE AROUND – AND ULTIMATELY LED THEM TO TITLE GLORY

You wouldn't expect it based on his monumental Hall of Fame career, but David Robinson was a late bloomer. He was active in sports as a child and teenager, but showed little talent or promise when it came to basketball. The then-5-foot 9-inches tall Robinson tried out for his high-school team but didn't stick with it. It wasn't until his senior year of high school, when he had sprouted up to 6-feet 6-inches that his coach coaxed him back onto the basketball court.

This time, he stuck with it, but it wasn't until his university years in the Naval Academy that he started turning into a real prospect. After a quiet freshman season, the still-growing Robinson exploded onto the scene as a sophomore, and came to dominate college basketball in a way no Navy player had done before. By the time he graduated, he had grown to a towering 7-feet tall, averaged 28 points per game in his senior season, and was promptly selected first overall in the 1987 NBA draft by the rebuilding San Antonio Spurs. The Spurs had been a dominant ABA team in the 1970s, but had struggled to stay in the upper echelons of the NBA since the ABA-NBA merger in 1976. Robinson was supposed to change all that. But the Spurs, and Robinson, would have to wait. Military rules dictated that Robinson would have to serve five years in the Navy after graduation, but this was commuted to two years after he was granted special dispensation. After two long years, where Robinson wasn't allowed to play any competitive basketball, he finally made his NBA debut in the 1989–90 season. The patience paid off immediately, as Robinson dominated the year's rookie class on his way to a Rookie of the Year award and the Spurs improved from 21 wins in 1988–89 to 56 wins and a trip to the Western Conference Semifinals.

The next year, Robinson led the league in rebounding, with 13.0 per game, while adding 25.6 points and 3.9 blocks per game. The year after that, he led the league in blocks and was

David Robinson brought flair, talent and title aspirations to the San Antonio Spurs

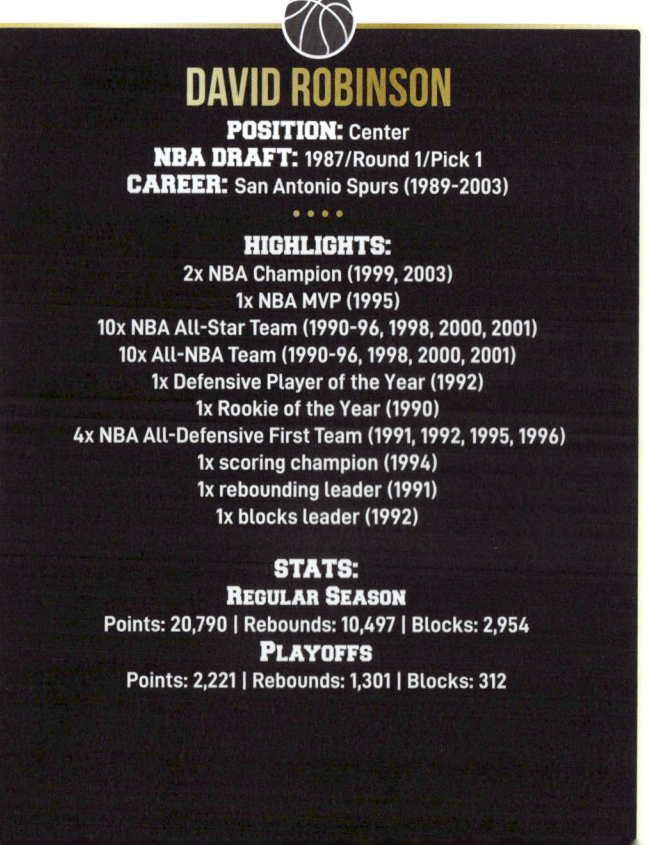

### DAVID ROBINSON
**POSITION:** Center
**NBA DRAFT:** 1987/Round 1/Pick 1
**CAREER:** San Antonio Spurs (1989-2003)

####  HIGHLIGHTS:
2x NBA Champion (1999, 2003)
1x NBA MVP (1995)
10x NBA All-Star Team (1990-96, 1998, 2000, 2001)
10x All-NBA Team (1990-96, 1998, 2000, 2001)
1x Defensive Player of the Year (1992)
1x Rookie of the Year (1990)
4x NBA All-Defensive First Team (1991, 1992, 1995, 1996)
1x scoring champion (1994)
1x rebounding leader (1991)
1x blocks leader (1992)

#### STATS:
**REGULAR SEASON**
Points: 20,790 | Rebounds: 10,497 | Blocks: 2,954
**PLAYOFFS**
Points: 2,221 | Rebounds: 1,301 | Blocks: 312

# DAVID ROBINSON | 105

Robinson was a powerful defender and ferocious shot-blocker

Robinson celebrates his second title in 2003 after his last-ever NBA game

## GOING FOR SCORING GOLD

### ON THE LAST DAY OF THE 1993-94 SEASON, ROBINSON ENTERED THE HISTORY BOOKS...

During the 1993-94 season, Robinson found himself in a tight battle with Orlando Magic center Shaquille O'Neal for the scoring title. On the final day of the season, 24 April, they were almost tied for the lead, and with a 32-point game by Shaq, Robinson needed to score 36 points or more against the Los Angeles Clippers to win the title.

He did just that – and then some – on his way to NBA history. In a mega-rare offensive display, Robinson scored a dizzying 71 points in a 112-97 victory, making 26 of 41 shots from the field, including a three-pointer, and 18 of 25 from the free-throw line. No other player on the Spurs team scored more than eight points in the game, but somehow, Robinson also tallied five assists in the game. This scoring outburst pushed his season average up to 29.8. Only five other players have ever topped the 70-point mark in NBA history, Elgin Baylor, Devin Booker, Kobe Bryant (who scored 81), David Thompson and Wilt Chamberlain.

voted the Defensive Player of the Year. What was missing, however, was postseason success. First round exits in 1991 and 1992 were followed by a second round bow in 1993 and a regression to a defeat in the first round in 1994. The Spurs struggled to construct the right supporting cast around the towering Robinson, whose individual brilliance could only carry the team so far in the hyper-competitive West.

Things seemed to turn a corner in 1994-95, when Robinson led the Spurs to the Western Conference Finals in a season where he won the MVP award after averaging 27.6 points and 10.8 rebounds per game. However, they were beaten by the Houston Rockets and Robinson's nemesis Hakeem Olajuwon, and a year later Robinson could only lead his Spurs to the Conference Semifinals, where the Utah Jazz vanquished them in six games.

Early in the 1996-97 season, injury struck, when Robinson broke his foot and sat out the rest of the season. But as fate would have it, that injury turned out to be a blessing in disguise both for the Spurs and Robinson's legacy. Having the top pick in the 1997 draft, San Antonio selected Tim Duncan, finally bringing Robinson the elite running mate he needed to make a run at the NBA title. After returning from injury, Robinson was happy to play second fiddle to the supremely talented Duncan, averaging 15.8 points and 10 rebounds per game in 1998-99. In the playoffs, Robinson replicated those numbers almost exactly, tallying 15.6 points and 9.9 rebounds per game as the Spurs ploughed through their opposition on the way to a dominant title. In the 1999 playoffs, the Spurs lost only two games.

Robinson and Duncan failed to retain the title, but did manage to regain it before Robinson's retirement. In 2002-03, a 37-year-old Robinson played more of a backup role than before, averaging 8.5 points in the regular season and 7.8 in the postseason, but he turned back the clock one last time in the title-clinching Game 6 against the New Jersey Nets. Scoring 13 points to go along with 17 rebounds and two blocks, it was a fitting ending to a career of patience and perseverance for David Robinson.

David Robinson edged Shaquille O'Neal for the 1993-94 scoring title

**"THINGS SEEMED TO TURN A CORNER IN 1994-95, WHEN ROBINSON LED THE SPURS TO THE WESTERN CONFERENCE FINALS"**

## NBA LEGENDS

# THE GAME CHANGER

### MADE IN GERMANY, BELOVED IN DALLAS, NOTHING WAS LOST IN TRANSLATION AS EUROPE'S GREATEST NBA EXPORT REDEFINED BASKETBALL

The ninth pick in the 1998 NBA draft, Dirk Nowitzki subsequently specialised in collecting firsts.

The leader of Dallas Mavericks as they won their first and only NBA championship. The first ever European to start an NBA All-Star Game. The first and only player to remain with a single NBA team for 21 seasons. And most significantly of all, the first player from the old continent to receive the NBA's Most Valuable Player award. His achievements were all the more remarkable due to the fact that he considered quitting the league due to homesickness during his rookie season.

It seemed astonishing then that this fish out of water – and seemingly out of his depth – could eventually morph into an all-time great in the jersey of the Dallas Mavericks, one who would both redefine his position and also the perception of the Europeans who followed in his wake. His journey led the sport down a bright new path. Others, as a consequence, scrambled to follow. But how was he moulded?

Many believe he entered the NBA draft with no notable pedigree. Minimal advance fame in the USA, perhaps. Previously, he had spent four years with his hometown club DJK Würzburg, and in his last season he was the MVP of the German Bundesliga.

However, in the pre-YouTube era, this was not enough to earn all-important buzz. But it hinted at an upward trajectory that properly accelerated in his mid-teens.

The DNA was solid. His mother Helga was a professional basketball player who represented her country in European finals. His father Jörg did the same in handball. Their son possessed the requisite height.

Firstly, his talents needed refinement. Individual coaching day after day from his mentor, Holger Geschwindner, turned rough edges into smooth skills. Still, both knew they had to counter perception and bias. Europeans, according to accepted NBA wisdom, were 'soft'. One-dimensional too. Not, by any stretch, equal to their American peers.

Geschwindner needed a way to prove his currency. The annual Nike Hoop Summit pitted the best teens of the United States against their international peers. Nowitzki, securing an invite, scored 33 points in his personal coming-out party. No longer could he be ignored.

The Mavericks' scouting crew, led by their coach, Don Nelson, and his son Donnie, liked the look of what they described as a "long, tall, skinny German drink of water". Their fans were less enthralled with the wunderkind. The boos on the

Nowitzki celebrates victory over the San Antonio Spurs during the 2014 playoffs

### DIRK NOWITZKI
**POSITION:** Power Forward
**NBA DRAFT:** 1998/Round 1/Pick 9
**CAREER:** Dallas Mavericks (1998-2019)

#### HIGHLIGHTS:
1x NBA Champion (2011)
1x NBA MVP (2007)
1x NBA Finals MVP (2011)
14x NBA All-Star Team (2002-12, 2014, 2015, 2019)
12x All-NBA Team (2001-12)

#### STATS:
**REGULAR SEASON**
Points: 31,560 | Rebounds: 11,489 | Assists: 3,651

**PLAYOFFS**
Points: 3,663 | Rebounds: 1,446 | Assists: 360

Nowitzki goes to the basket in Game 6 of the 2006 NBA Finals in which the Mavericks would come up short

"NOWITZKI SCORED 33 POINTS IN HIS PERSONAL COMING-OUT PARTY. NO LONGER COULD HE BE IGNORED"

# NBA LEGENDS

Nowitzki announced his retirement in 2019 after 21 seasons with the Mavericks

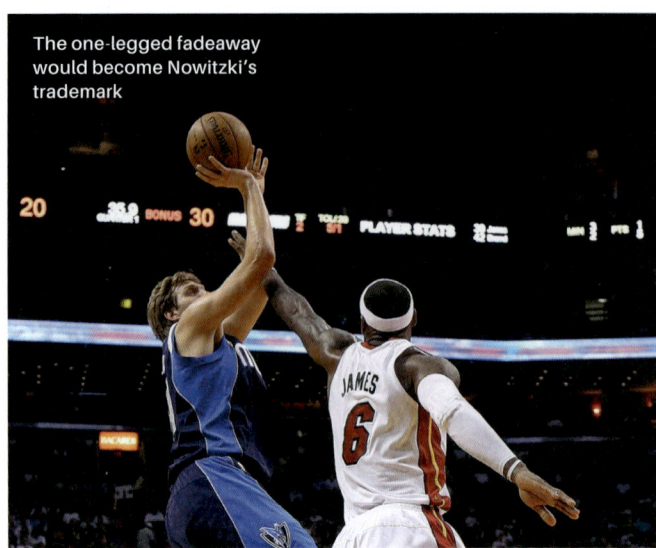

The one-legged fadeaway would become Nowitzki's trademark

## "A DEADLOCK AT 2-2. AND FROM THEN ON, IT BECAME HIS SERIES – AND HIS CHAMPIONSHIP"

draft night of 1998 rang loudly when a trade was executed with the Milwaukee Bucks to acquire the unheralded rookie. Additionally, they signed up Steve Nash, a duo that looked more like The Beach Boys than hoops heroes in the making. A gamble, it seemed.

"We had literally thrown our reputations, history, everything we've done in the league in the hands of two young guys that were completely unproven," Donnie conceded. "A lot of times, those guys have kind of a high casualty count. Especially guys from Europe. So it was exhilarating, fun and frightening, all at the same time."

The future MVPs bonded. In Nelson, Nowitzki had a coach who gave him a licence to shoot rather than edicts to follow. The Mavs, so long strugglers, did not gain an instant lift. The hecklers screamed. The veterans of the league sensed blood. A band-aid was quickly applied.

In his second year, he was runner-up in the NBA's Most Improved Player stakes. His numbers shot up exponentially, joining Nash and Michael Finley in an exciting Big Three in the Big D. His one-legged fadeaway jumper would become his trademark. Others rushed to make their own copies. And although his running mates would depart, Nowitzki's stature grew and grew.

The Mavericks reached the 2006 NBA Finals. A 2-0 lead was opened up against the Miami Heat. The advantage, though, soon evaporated.

Management sequestered the entire team in a hotel, but Nowitzki's reliable three-point shooting went AWOL. He missed chances, which proved fatal as the Heat blew by. Questions, again questions. Were foreign players lacking?

Recalled Donnie Nelson: "You hear things like, 'you'll never be able to win a championship with someone with a European mentality'. 'They don't understand our game'. 'There's no defense, people won't follow that kind of a leader'.

"Blah blah blah. This and that. You hear everything. And when you fail, those things, whether they're real or not, become true in people's minds. And so when we're sitting there, about to stick a flag into Mount Everest in our first Finals run, and that cup is literally ripped from our arms, then you hear all of the naysayers."

Stung, the German retreated to the Australian Outback to heal. His hair ever longer, his beard more ragged, he refined himself. Averaging 24.6 points and 8.9 rebounds, leading the Mavericks to 67 wins and number one seed in the Western Conference, he would acquire the MVP trophy at the close of the subsequent campaign.

This was bittersweet ultimately, with Dallas ousted from the playoffs by the eight-seeded Golden State Warriors in a momentous upset. Four years passed until another crack at the title. 2011, the Miami Heat, once again. LeBron James, Chris Bosh and Dwyane Wade fronted the super-team in opposition.

In Game 1, Nowitzki injured his finger. There was no danger he would not return. Next game, he ignited a rally that levelled the series at 1-1. In Game 3, Miami survived when his late shot fell short. During Game 4, he had to ignore a 38°C fever. Still, he converted the winning basket. A deadlock at 2-2. And from then on, it became his series – and his championship. For his sublime showing, averaging 26 points and 9.7 rebounds, he was named the Finals MVP.

Catharsis and redemption for 2006. "That was one of my

*After a difficult start to life in the US, Nowitzki would go on to become a firm fans' favourite in Dallas*

Spurs. He had 20 points and ten rebounds before bidding farewell, leaving as the only player to have picked up at least 31,000 points, 10,000 rebounds, 3,000 assists, 1,000 steals, 1,000 blocks and 1,000 two-point field goals in NBA history. Not many players walk away from basketball knowing they've reshaped the game. In Dallas, few have ever been so beloved.

A wizard from Würzburg. A titan in Texas. An ambassador for Europe and a trailblazer who proved big men can shoot from anywhere at any time.

most disappointing losses in my career, to lose the final series after being up 2-0," Nowitzki said. "It took so long just to get here. I don't really know if it would have made a difference. Just this feeling, to be on the best team of the world, is just indescribable.

"That's why this is extra special. If I would have won one early in my career, maybe I would have never put all the work and the time in that I have over the last 13 years. So this is amazing."

Try saying now that Europeans can't ball. Perceptions were altered forever. In Germany, they felt only pride. Their favourite son had stamped the country firmly on the basketball map. For his national team too, he shipped home his ethic and drive.

Never previously an international powerhouse, the Germans landed an unprecedented bronze medal at the 2002 FIBA World Championships in Indianapolis. Top scoring with 24 points per game Nowitzki, was the tournament's MVP.

Missing out on the 2004 Olympics following an injury to their star, Germany reached the following summer's EuroBasket Final, losing to Greece. Another MVP prize for Dirk.

To finally gain a shot at an Olympics meant surviving a single qualification game against Puerto Rico. Nowitzki's game-high 32 points secured a ticket to Beijing in 2008. At the opening ceremony, the country's export to Texas carried Deutschland's flag. "I never thought I would be chosen," he admitted. "Maybe it's happened because a lot of athletes identify with me." Germany would finish tenth. Dirk relished every moment.

The latter stage of his career brought more records and accomplishments until he retired in 2019. His last season would bring his 14th All-Star appearance. He would leave the league as its sixth-highest scoring player of all time.

Never one to seek the spotlight, he did not confirm his exit until after his final home game, which saw him score 30 points. The end of the line came a day later against the San Antonio

## THE DIRK WHISPERER

### HOLGER GESCHWINDNER TRANSFORMED DIRK NOWITZKI FROM A LONG SHOT TO A SURE THING

"Without him," the NBA legend told *Der Spiegel*, "I might be a boring businessman or a painter in my parents' company."

The former captain of Germany was the first to spot the extraordinary potential that might be realised, approaching him after a youth game when he was 16 and offering to become a personal mentor.

The agreement was that they were not striving to create someone who could merely shine in their homeland. The mission was to conquer the NBA. Hence, Nowitzki's shooting technique was mechanically broken down and rebuilt through daily drills, invented from scratch. Balance, leg movement, footwork – all engrained.

It created something boldly unique. "In those days, the big guys were allowed to shoot from an inch away from the basket," Geschwindner recounted to *Slam*. "There was never a big guy that could shoot a three-pointer. So I told Dirk that if we wanted to have a chance, we need to catch their attention."

It did, and the rest is history. And theirs was a relationship that endured with teacher and pupil regularly convening through Nowitzki's career, in season and in summers, to maintain the education. Time in the classroom very well spent.

*Nowitzki alongside his mentor Holger Geschwindner*

# NBA LEGENDS

# THE CHAMPION SUPREME

### THE BOSTON CELTICS OF THE 1950S AND 1960S CHASED TITLES RELENTLESSLY. THEIR TOWERING TOTEM REMAINS THE ULTIMATE WINNER

There have been great winners in professional basketball. Champions, supreme players who made unique marks in history. None, though, achieved as much as Bill Russell. His was a career for the ages, one in which triumph was a staple and accomplishments an absurd norm.

Eleven times an NBA champion as a player, including twice as a player-coach, a tally unsurpassed. Five times the NBA's Most Valuable Player. And an Olympic gold medal thrown on top for good measure.

Statistics simply cannot tell the full story of Russell's extraordinary impact, both during a playing career with the Boston Celtics and also off the court as a role model for African-Americans during an era in which the racial conflicts and societal shifts across the USA engulfed the world of sport.

Born in Louisiana and later growing up in California, Russell experienced poverty and racism in a land that did not appear to offer equal opportunity. His athleticism offered an escape route. A talented high jumper, he decided that basketball should become the beneficiary of his immense gifts. Growing to 6-feet 10-inches tall, he was offered a scholarship to the University of San Francisco where his raw talent was sculpted into polished performances and renown as an imposing enforcer. Two NCAA championships were secured. As the 1956 NBA draft approached, Boston's coach Red Auerbach coveted a streak of toughness which this starlet might inject. The St Louis Hawks held the second pick. As he did so often, Auerbach pulled off a trade that would work in his favour, the Celtics acquiring a rookie who would become their fulcrum during two decades of unparalleled dominance.

Prior to his arrival, Russell competed for the USA at the 1956

Russell goes up for a block against the LA Lakers' Jerry West

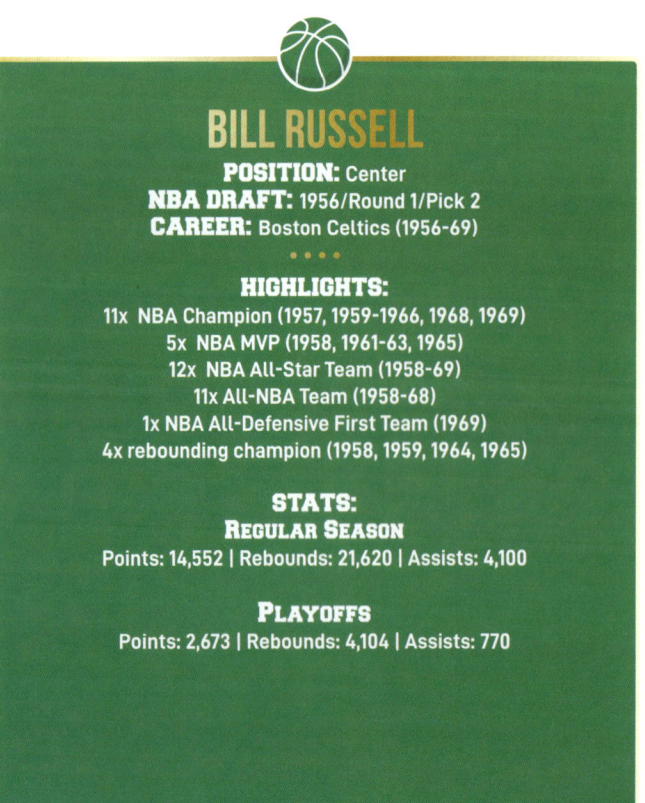

### BILL RUSSELL
**POSITION:** Center
**NBA DRAFT:** 1956/Round 1/Pick 2
**CAREER:** Boston Celtics (1956-69)

**HIGHLIGHTS:**
11x NBA Champion (1957, 1959-1966, 1968, 1969)
5x NBA MVP (1958, 1961-63, 1965)
12x NBA All-Star Team (1958-69)
11x All-NBA Team (1958-68)
1x NBA All-Defensive First Team (1969)
4x rebounding champion (1958, 1959, 1964, 1965)

**STATS:**
**REGULAR SEASON**
Points: 14,552 | Rebounds: 21,620 | Assists: 4,100

**PLAYOFFS**
Points: 2,673 | Rebounds: 4,104 | Assists: 770

Olympic Games in Melbourne. He was instrumental in guiding the Americans to gold by beating the Soviet Union 89-55 in the final, with their center averaging a team-high 14.1 points per game. It was the perfect warm-up for his NBA career. Entering the league that winter, he joined a roster which already included numerous future Hall of Famers: Tommy Heinsohn, Bill Sharman and Bob Cousy. From his very debut, Russell became the foundation, a one-man blocking machine who became the first to average 20 rebounds per game in a season.

Within seven months, he would become an NBA champion as well, the Hawks vanquished in a deciding Game 7 which was only decided after double overtime. The first of the Celtics' record 17 titles. The celebration provided a taste of success that Russell would consume, over and over again.

Ten times within the next 12 years, in fact, in an era of unmatched domination. Challengers would threaten, notably the LA Lakers, who were the fall guys in the Finals seven times as a rivalry was stoked. Wilt Chamberlain, the antithesis of Russell as a free-wheeling scoring machine, would sneak just one past his illustrious counterpart when the Philadelphia 76ers prevailed in 1967.

Mere blips. Big Bill continued to rack up enduring numbers of his own. 12 times an NBA All-Star. Thrice a member of the All-NBA First Team. Four times the league's rebounding champion, averaging 15.1 points and an astonishing 22.5 rebounds during his playing career on a team for the ages.

He was fortunate that Auerbach offered constant reinforcements. Cousy retired. John Havlicek arrived. The bandwagon continued. Russell consistently driving his colleagues on. "You got to have the killer instinct," he underlined. "If you do not have it, forget about basketball and go into social psychology or something. If you sometimes wonder if you've got it, you ain't got it. No pussycats, please."

Opinionated and vocal in his evaluations, he was not liked by all. Yet few would deny him complete respect. When Auerbach vacated the bench, his center took over, completing the final three seasons of his career as a rarity: a player-coach. Twice under his mentorship, the Celtics added to his championship haul. However the double role wore him down. The volatile politics of the country, he admitted, became an additional distraction. Yet he would summon one last effort. At age 35, he grabbed 21 rebounds in a concluding victory in the 1969 NBA Finals over a Lakers team which included Chamberlain.

Days later, he announced his retirement in a magazine and dramatically severed all ties. A fractious farewell to a city which he felt had not properly embraced people of colour.

> **"YOU GOT TO HAVE THE KILLER INSTINCT. IF YOU DO NOT HAVE IT, FORGET ABOUT BASKETBALL. IF YOU SOMETIMES WONDER IF YOU'VE GOT IT, YOU AIN'T GOT IT"**

Russell holds back his great rival Wilt Chamberlain during a fiery encounter between the Celtics and the 76ers

## AN ACTIVIST UNDER ATTACK
### RUSSELL COULDN'T ESCAPE THE RACISM THAT PLAGUED BOSTON

Bill Russell's position as the NBA's first black coach was merely one of many points where the thorny issue of race traversed his life...

And it led to an active role in the Civil Rights Movement. As a child in the segregated city of Monroe, he witnessed inequality at first hand. In basketball too. While some teams openly baulked at the idea of signing African-American recruits, the Celtics had broken down the colour bar by acquiring Chuck Cooper. Society, around them, was slower to evolve. On one occasion, he and his black teammates were forced to stay in a separate hotel in still-segregated Charlotte. Restaurants, on the road, refused their business. Ironically it was in Boston where he often felt least welcome. "A flea market of racism," he called it. Increasingly militant, Russell retained a dignified defiance. But he stopped signing autographs with Boston's fans and withdrew from speaking to the media as the mutual antipathy grew. Jarringly, his home was vandalised and tarred with racist epitaphs. "Not only am I tall enough to make a lot of people uncomfortable," he said, "but I am also black, and infamous as an athlete." Even immense success could not insulate him.

Russell (front left) alongside Muhammad Ali and other African-American sports stars, including Kareem Abdul-Jabbar

# THE QUIET ASSASSIN

### A MAN OF FEW WORDS, TIM DUNCAN INSTEAD LET HIS MAJESTIC GAME DO THE TALKING IN SAN ANTONIO

We inhabit a world, driven by social media, in which the winners are often believed to be those who make the most noise. Tim Duncan will take a pass.

He does not belong in such a rowdy and random universe. Better to show rather than tell, he suggests. To let actions speak much louder than words. Unquestionably the most accomplished power forward that basketball has ever seen, you suspect Duncan would have chosen to excel behind closed doors if such an option had existed. Begrudgingly, the world was allowed to witness his greatness on show, night after night as the San Antonio Spurs earned five NBA titles during his career. The most private of superstars was a vocal leader during their quests. Off the court, he spoke only when absolutely required.

What a contrast the Virgin Islander was to so many of his peers. He did not seek attention. In fact, when it approached, he bolted rapidly in the other direction. A joker and a loyal teammate, a compulsive video gamer and car junkie, he offered few glimpses of his world outside the locker room.

That poker face rarely dropped. Celebrity was a foreign language. "If I were to psychoanalyse myself," he declared in a rare moment of insight, "I'd have to say I am a clown, cleverly disguised as a regular person." An enigma for those who chronicled his career, but foremost to his opponents. His Hall of Fame CV was not built around flashy passes or high-flying dunks. But in something altogether more mundane: pure, simple fundamentals. All that was required. "You don't see Timmy beating his chest as if he was the first human being to hug the basketball, as a lot of people do these days," his Spurs head coach for his entire career, Gregg Popovich, praised. "He's not pointing to the sky. He's not glamming to the cameras. He just plays."

In a parallel universe, Duncan might have never entered the global consciousness at all. A wind which blew across his island paradise altered his path. During his teens. Duncan sought to be an athlete at the highest level. But swimming was his sport of choice. His elder sister, Tricia, had competed at an Olympics for the US Virgin Islands. Her sibling had similar ambitions, quick enough in the freestyle to believe that he could represent the US.

However in 1989, Hurricane Hugo ripped up the only Olympic swimming pool nearby. Swimming amongst the sharks in the ocean did not carry the same easy appeal. Basketball proved a more than adequate athletic replacement. And having promised his late mother that he would earn a college degree, the opportunity to go to Wake Forest University in North Carolina provided him with an outlet to utilise his considerable intellect and his towering frame.

> "HE'S NOT POINTING TO THE SKY. HE'S NOT GLAMMING TO THE CAMERAS. HE JUST PLAYS"

Kobe Bryant battles for possession with Duncan during the 2008 playoffs

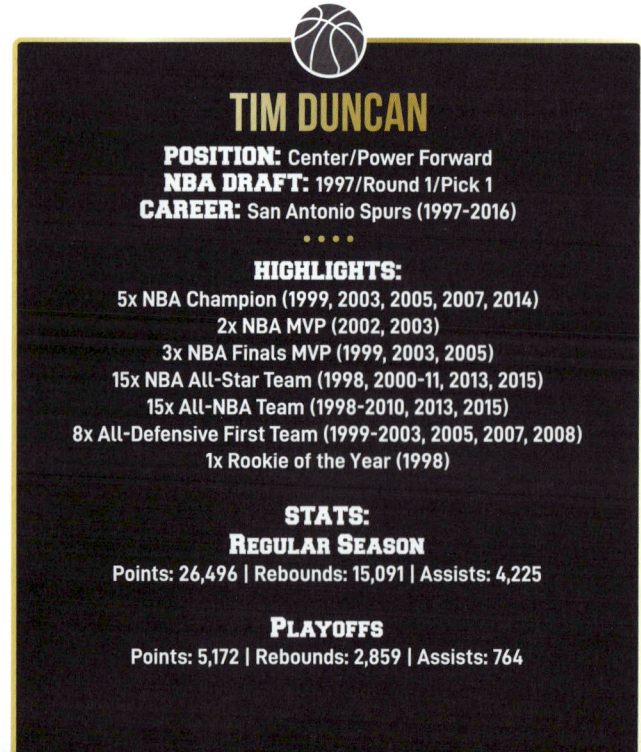

## TIM DUNCAN

**POSITION:** Center/Power Forward
**NBA DRAFT:** 1997/Round 1/Pick 1
**CAREER:** San Antonio Spurs (1997-2016)

### HIGHLIGHTS:
5x NBA Champion (1999, 2003, 2005, 2007, 2014)
2x NBA MVP (2002, 2003)
3x NBA Finals MVP (1999, 2003, 2005)
15x NBA All-Star Team (1998, 2000-11, 2013, 2015)
15x All-NBA Team (1998-2010, 2013, 2015)
8x All-Defensive First Team (1999-2003, 2005, 2007, 2008)
1x Rookie of the Year (1998)

### STATS:
**REGULAR SEASON**
Points: 26,496 | Rebounds: 15,091 | Assists: 4,225

**PLAYOFFS**
Points: 5,172 | Rebounds: 2,859 | Assists: 764

## TIM DUNCAN

Duncan dunks on Mike Conley of the Memphis Grizzlies during the 2013 playoffs

# NBA LEGENDS

Spurs coach Gregg Popovich (right) built his best championship teams around the dominance of Duncan

## "DUNCAN BECAME ONLY THE SECOND PLAYER TO WIN A CHAMPIONSHIP IN THREE SEPARATE DECADES"

An anomaly by remaining on campus for a full four years, he became the leading rebounder in NCAA history. No wonder that when he completed his studies in 1997, few doubted he would be picked first in the NBA draft.

The Spurs held that golden ticket after an injury-plagued previous year. They could quickly rebound into contention with a young star. Slotting Duncan in beside David Robinson, the 'Twin Towers' were constructed.

Immediately impactful, Duncan made the first of his 15 All-Star appearances in his rookie year. And in his second, greater gains would come. The Spurs launched themselves toward the 1999 NBA Finals against the New York Knicks. In Game 5, Duncan dropped 31 points, and nine rebounds to secure a 4-1 series victory.

The Spurs' first-ever championship – with Duncan the Finals MVP. "Back in the locker room, I was two seconds away from just breaking down," he confessed. A rare admission of an emotional switch.

Titles became an addictive habit. After consecutive NBA Most Valuable Player honours, San Antonio defeated the New Jersey Nets 4-2 in the 2003 Finals with Duncan approaching a quadruple-double in the closer. Another MVP. Extra plaudits.

And when Robinson retired, it became his team with Tony Parker and Manu Ginóbili his formidable accomplices in a Big Three. In 2005, the Detroit Pistons would end as their vanquished foes in an NBA Finals decided in a seventh contest. Duncan, the catalyst, had 25 points and 11 rebounds in the decider. A third Finals MVP collected. Only the fourth player ever to be a three-time recipient. Try as they might, the Spurs would never quite procure back-to-back titles but they cemented a dynastic run. In 2007, San Antonio swept the Cleveland Cavaliers and the young star LeBron James 4-0. "The best" of my titles,

said Duncan. Seven years passed until the confetti would fall again. It concluded a revenge mission. In 2013, the Spurs had squared off with the then-reigning champions, the Miami Heat, and seemed poised for a championship celebration as Game 6 neared its end. Improbably, in overtime, the champagne was left on ice, even with their colossus gathering 30 points and 17 rebounds. The Heat repeated by winning Game 7.

Duncan's competitive ire silently burned. "It left a bad taste in our mouths." The rematch arrived 12 months later. A no-contest in the end, a 4-1 Spurs triumph. 38-year-old Duncan became only the second player to win a championship in three separate decades, this time with a youthful Kawhi Leonard as MVP.

As his prime seemed set to pass, Duncan continued to quietly excel. His attitude varied little at either bookend of his NBA spell. "Basketball's so much like life: if something's going great, you wait a minute, it will change," he declared. "If something's going bad, you wait a minute, it will change. So I try to play things on such an even keel, knowing that things are going to change. You take the good with the bad.

"You don't get too excited, you don't get too down. And sometimes that's the hardest thing in the world to do when you're in the midst of it. But that's the best way to handle it."

Never reliant on athleticism but on deft footwork, nimble movement and an admirable dedication to defense, he was able to parlay his adherence to the fundamentals into extending the Spurs playoff streak over a longer span than ever accomplished before.

Remarkably, even with mounting knee issues, his numbers remained solid despite the fact he was approaching his 40th year. His sole Achilles' heel was his foul shooting. Everything else? Pretty superior. Only on the international stage did he underachieve. He fulfilled his Olympic ambition in Athens in 2004 but an underwhelming US squad managed only bronze following an unprecedented three losses. Even adding two FIBA Americas titles

Duncan blocks a layup by Goran Dragic of the Phoenix Suns

Duncan drives towards the basket during Game 4 of the Western Conference Semifinals in 2004

# TIM DUNCAN

## THE SPURS WAY

### THE CULTURE OF THE SAN ANTONIO SPURS IS THE ENVY OF FRIENDS AND FOES

So much so, that their structure has become the model to emulate. Team, before individual. Unity prized but also self-expression permitted.

At its epicentre remains Gregg Popovich, a second father as much as head coach. "Hug 'em and hold 'em," he always asserted was his approach to his players, cultivated over dinners and wine on the road and conversations about family, politics, history and a world outside the narrow confines of the NBA.

Over a streak of five titles in 15 years, it fiercely bonded the Spurs together. For their enlarged contingent of foreign recruits, San Antonio easily felt a home away from home.

Ultimately, there remained a relentless impetus from Popovich to push his team to improve and compete. And while the potency of such a message might normally dull over time, that Tim Duncan followed his lead did most to keep the culture intact.

As Tony Parker wrote: "You see this all-world player, this All-NBA First Team, MVP of the Finals, about to be MVP of the league guy, and here he is in practice, willing to be coached like he's fighting for a spot on the team. It was unreal."

The 'Twin Towers' of Tim Duncan and David Robinson won two championships together

did not persuade Duncan that this was his sphere.

San Antonio provided all the enrichment he could ever need. A perfect foil for Popovich, their shared vision was to enjoy life and relish victories, large and small, rather than to generate unnecessary hype. A love story, of sorts, between two men with little desire to please anyone other than themselves and those for whom they truly cared.

"His willingness to allow me and my staff to coach him, and coach him critically, 'you did well, you did poorly, here's the deal,' that allowed for a lot of success. Because that set the tone for every other player that's ever come through that door. Because when somebody like him accepts and wants direction and coaching, and responds to it so well, it makes it very difficult for anybody else to go in a different direction. So that was huge for our success," said Pop.

It is typical of Duncan that when he announced his retirement in 2016, it was not trumpeted via a press conference beamed live to the nation, but via the blandest of press releases and zero fanfare. Substance over hype. The right play over the highlight play, boring his rivals into submission if need be with repeated displays of uncomplicated excellence.

Silence, he felt, was an undervalued virtue. Even if his performances spoke volumes and glittered and dazzled in ways no words could possibly convey.

# NBA LEGENDS

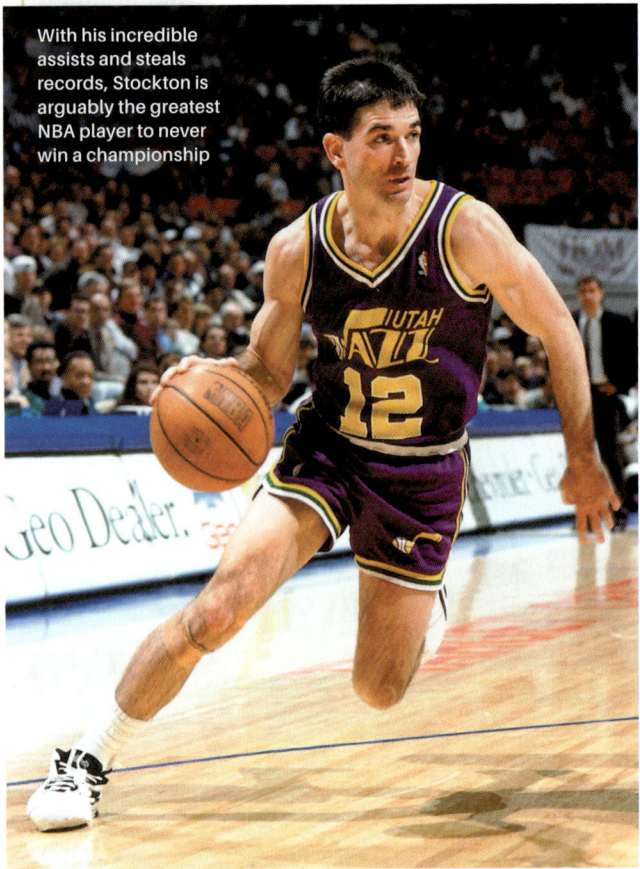

With his incredible assists and steals records, Stockton is arguably the greatest NBA player to never win a championship

"STOCKTON'S BATTLING NATURE, CRAFTY GAMESMANSHIP AND UNDERSTANDING OF THE GAME HELPED HIM TO BE A THORN IN EVERY OPPOSING ATTACKER'S SIDE"

# NBA'S NEARLY MAN

### SO NEAR BUT YET SO FAR IS A PHRASE THAT SUMS UP ONE OF THE SPORT'S GREATEST, BUT UNLUCKIEST, STARS: JOHN STOCKTON

Some sporting legends have bulging trophy cabinets. Some have rafts of personal accolades. Some are born showpeople whose personalities and skills earn them countless endorsements and autobiography sales. But some – like John Stockton – have none of these, which makes his elevation to legend status all the more remarkable.

Washington-born Stockton had an impressive high school and college basketball career, but few predicted the remarkable NBA career that was to follow. Stockton was drafted 16th overall by Utah Jazz in 1984, behind the likes of Hakeem Olajuwon, Michael Jordan and Charles Barkley. Jazz were an emerging force in the competition, their 1984 playoff spot the first in their ten years of existence. But the point guard made them a consistent force to be reckoned with, helping the team to reach the playoffs in every one of his 19 seasons in the NBA. But, sadly, they never won the title, thwarted twice at the final hurdle by Jordan's Chicago Bulls.

Stockton appeared in all 82 games during his rookie season, but started just five as he battled to depose the Jazz's first-choice point guard Rickey Green. However, he helped his side to a second consecutive postseason appearance, losing out to the Denver Nuggets.

His influence on the Jazz steadily increased over the next few seasons until he was an undroppable part of the team, starting all 82 games of the season on an incredible 12 occasions, including his final four seasons in the NBA. A 41-year-old playing at the highest level is almost unheard of, but for him to be an integral part of a side that was regularly making the postseason shows what a true giant of the game Stockton was.

Stockton was a defensive machine, the only man to have made over 3,000 steals in the NBA, despite his relatively short stature. He was a fiery competitor and his battling nature, crafty gamesmanship and understanding of the game helped him to be a thorn in every opposing attacker's side. As well as dominating on defense, Stockton was also the ultimate assist-maker. With a quick eye, large hands and tricky-to-pick single-handed, push-style pass, Stockton set up over 15,800 baskets

# JOHN STOCKTON

Stockton and Karl Malone (right) were the masters of the pick-and-roll move

## GOING FOR GOLD
### STOCKTON'S CAREER WASN'T ALL DOOM AND GLOOM AS TWO ICONIC BITS OF BLING SHOW

While an NBA championship ring was just about kept out of Mr Clutch's clutches, John Stockton did have two very precious team awards to adorn his mantlepiece upon his retirement from the sport.

The 1992 Barcelona Olympic Games saw the first USA basketball Dream Team compete in one of the quadrennial event's most incredible mismatches. This was the first year NBA players were able to be selected and the USA went for it – with Stockton chosen alongside the likes of Malone, Jordan, Johnson, Larry Bird and Patrick Ewing. USA steamrollered their way to gold, with their 117-85 gold medal match victory over Croatia their smallest winning margin. Stockton's presence on that team, despite having just recovered from a broken leg, showed the high regard he was kept in – and his longevity was proven four years later when he made the squad again, aged 34. He was one of only five players to be reselected, alongside Malone, Barkley, Scottie Pippen and David Robinson. The USA were less dominant but still cruised every match by at least 22 points, earning Stockton his second Olympic gold.

The USA's Dream Team blew away the opposition to win Olympic gold in 1992

for his teammates, an NBA record and nearly 4,000 more than his nearest challenger. His average of 10.5 assists per game is bettered only by Magic Johnson – a man who had the NBA all-time points scorer Kareem Abdul-Jabbar to aim for.

Not that Stockton was a one-man team. In his second season he was joined by Karl Malone, a man who would go on to score nearly 37,000 points – second only behind Abdul-Jabbar. "Stockton to Malone" was a phrase that commentators might as well have had pre-recorded as the two formed one of the competition's all-time deadliest partnerships. The two had an incredible relationship on the court and to this day it remains one of life's enduring mysteries as to how neither of them ended up with a championship ring on their finger.

Stockton's Jazz reached the Conference Finals three times during the 1990s, until finally in 1997 they reached their maiden NBA Finals. Stockton provided nearly nine assists per game and Malone fought valiantly, but they couldn't stop a ruthless Jordan-led Chicago Bulls victory. The following year, it was the same two teams in the Finals, and once again Jordan was unstoppable, top scoring in five of the six games as Jazz were dispatched 4-2 for a second year running.

Stockton continued to ply his relentless trade up and down the court into his fifth decade on the planet, but he and Malone couldn't guide Jazz back to a third Finals. So, in 2003, having still started every match that season, Stockton made his final appearance in a Jazz jersey. His number 12 was retired the following year and he was inducted into the Hall of Fame in 2009. After 19 years of playoff consistency, it was little surprise that the year after he hung up his sneakers, the team failed to make the playoffs.

He wasn't flashy but was widely acknowledged to be one of the hardest-working and talented players the league has ever seen. His records that still stand in the assists and steals categories demonstrate without a shadow of a doubt that he was one of the NBA's most selfless players. Stockton may not have the trophy cabinet of his peers, or the number of MVP awards, but no conversation about the all-time greatest point guard is complete without a nod to the talents of the Utah Jazz's John Stockton.

## JOHN STOCKTON
**POSITION:** Point Guard
**NBA DRAFT:** 1984/Round 1/Pick 16
**CAREER:** Utah Jazz 1984-2003

### HIGHLIGHTS:
10x NBA All-Star Team (1989-97, 2000)
11x All-NBA Team (1988-97, 1999)
9x assists leader (1988-96)
2x steals leader (1989, 1992)

### STATS:
**REGULAR SEASON**
Points: 19,711 | Assists: 15,806 | Steals: 3,265

**PLAYOFFS**
Points: 2,436 | Assists: 1,839 | Steals: 338

The Chicago Bulls celebrate their victory over the Seattle SuperSonics in the 1996 NBA Finals

# TOP 10 LEGENDARY TEAMS

### EVERY NBA SEASON ENDS WITH JUST ONE TEAM STILL STANDING, BUT WHILE ALL CHAMPIONS ARE SPECIAL, SOME ARE MORE SPECIAL THAN OTHERS

A legendary team is the product of many things. Teamwork is essential, because even the brightest talents can fall if they are not supported.

Great coaching is necessary to navigate a path through the long season, guarding against over-confidence when the wins are flowing and picking the team up after the inevitable defeats.

Star players still grab the headlines, and almost no team can reach the status of true legends without marquee names, but a select few manage to combine into something beyond a collection of glittering stars.

Judging teams from different eras is difficult, as the evolution of the game means that straight-up comparisons would nearly always come out in favour of the more modern squads, but teams can only fairly be judged against their contemporaries.

One more thing is essential. Winning an NBA title is necessary for inclusion in this group, which means that some wonderful teams (such as the Golden State Warriors of 2015-16) have to watch from the sidelines – but in a game of last man standing, only the very best can be considered legendary.

# THE UNSTOPPABULLS
# CHICAGO BULLS
## 1995–1996

Michael Jordan finished the 1995–1996 season as the league MVP, Finals MVP and NBA champion

Michael Jordan's brief flirtation with professional baseball had disrupted the Bulls, but his return in 1995 boosted the team into the playoffs once more. The following season, he was back to his best in what was arguably the greatest NBA team of all time.

The Bulls were far from a one-man team, and the addition of Dennis Rodman helped push them to the top. While Jordan and Scottie Pippen brought the flair, Rodman gave the team its edge. Some questioned whether such an abrasive character might wreck team harmony, but the big man himself had no doubts.

"Nothing gets to us," Rodman would say during the NBA Finals. "Nothing makes us lose our cool. Not even me. Everybody wants to say Dennis Rodman's crazy, but I'm not. Dennis Rodman knows exactly what he's doing."

The 1995–96 season would see Chicago win the first of three straight championships – the second time the franchise scored a 'three-peat'. After storming to a 41-3 record, the team eventually finished with a then-record 72 regular season wins. Jordan finished with a points-per-game average of over 30 for the eighth and last time in his career.

The Bulls were dominant in almost all phases. Jordan led the league in scoring and Rodman in rebounds. Just about the only category in which the team was not exceptional was in three-pointers. They sank 544 long-range shots during the season – tenth best in the league.

The Bulls also got major input from Luc Longley, Toni Kukoč, Ron Harper, Steve Kerr, Bill Wennington and Dickey Simpkins. Kukoč was especially influential, averaging 13.1 points per game, and his efforts were recognised when he won the 'Sixth Man of the Year' award.

Following their regular season fireworks, the Bulls were 15-3 in the playoffs. They were almost untouchable in the Eastern Conference playoffs, with their only loss in 12 games coming against the Knicks. They romped to a three-game lead in the Finals, weathered a two-game revival from the SuperSonics and then beat them handily in Game 6 to land the title.

# THE BAD BOYS
# DETROIT PISTONS
## 1988–1989

*The Pistons' Bill Laimbeer guards an opponent during Detroit's reign of terror*

They say that nice guys finish last. The 1988-89 Pistons had no intention of seeing if that held true on the basketball court. The Pistons revelled in their bad-boy image, seemingly more intent on destroying what the other team could do than creating anything themselves. It is a skewed image, of course – the Pistons may have favoured defense, but they could play in all phases of the game.

Dennis Rodman, John Salley and Bill Laimbeer (the pantomime villain in chief) set the tone for a gritty, blue-collar squad that was just unpleasant to play against. A total of 63 regular season wins could not have come from defense alone, but the team did not have a single player averaging 20 points per game. Instead, they spread the responsibility for keeping the scoreboard moving.

With Isiah Thomas providing their main offensive threat, the Pistons bullied their way to the Finals, and were in no mood to change their style of play once there, stifling the Lakers en route to a stunning 4-0 series sweep.

## NBA LEGENDS

# THE RECORD BREAKERS
# GOLDEN STATE WARRIORS
## 2016–2017

The Warriors of 2015–16 seemed destined to make this list, amassing a record 73 regular season wins, but defeat in the NBA Finals wrecked their bid. Just one year later, the mistake was rectified, and the Warriors lifted the title.

In the maelstrom of a fierce rivalry with Cleveland (the teams met in four consecutive finals from 2015 to 2018), the Warriors put up one of the most dominating regular seasons in memory, enjoying a huge +11.6 points differential over their opponents.

They then breezed through the playoffs, winning 16 out of 17 games (the best playoff record ever) and destroying the Cavaliers in the finals. Behind Draymond Green (Defensive Player of the Year) and the high-scoring trio of Stephen Curry, Kevin Durant and Klay Thompson, the Warriors were too hot to handle, winning 67 regular season games.

Kevin Durant in action during the Warriors' championship victory over the Cavaliers

# RECIPE FOR SUCCESS
# MILWAUKEE BUCKS
## 1970–1971

Kareem Abdul-Jabbar was part of a legendary team at the tail end of his career, with the Lakers in 1986–87, but it was nothing new for him. He had enjoyed the same experience 16 years earlier, with the Bucks.

Abdul-Jabbar (then still known as Lew Alcindor) was the star in Milwaukee from day one, and by his second season he was ready to spearhead a truly great team, averaging 31.7 points and 16 rebounds per game. Fellow second-year star Bob Dandridge, meanwhile, stepped up to be a formidable scorer as well.

The Bucks offered a masterclass in blending experience with youthful energy, matching their two precocious youngsters with an ageing veteran in Oscar Robertson, who arrived in the offseason. Robertson brought vast experience and an appetite to land the NBA championship that had so far eluded him. Although fading as a points scorer, he still excelled as a distributor.

With support from Jon McGlocklin, Bob Boozer and Greg Smith, the Bucks enjoyed a then-record 20-game winning streak and finished the regular season at 66-16. A one-sided Finals saw them sweep the Baltimore Bullets 4-0.

Oscar Roberston's veteran savvy was key for the Bucks in their championship run

# HOME SWEET HOME
## BOSTON CELTICS
## 1985-1986

Boston Garden was a terrible place for opposing teams to visit in the 1980s. In the 1985-86 season, they might as well not have bothered turning up. The Celtics went an incredible 40-1 at home on their way to a 67-15 regular season record.

Larry Bird was at the height of his powers, winning his third straight league MVP award and he teamed with Kevin McHale and Robert Parish to give Boston its feared 'Big Three'. Dennis Johnson, Bill Walton and Danny Ainge weighed in with important contributions as well (Walton snagged 544 rebounds, while Johnson and Ainge averaged 15.6 and 10.7 points per game respectively).

But it was the peerless Bird who was the beating heart of the team, leading the Celtics in scoring, assists, rebounds and steals. Only one game was dropped in the Eastern Conference playoffs as the Bulls (despite Michael Jordan scoring 63 points in Game 2 of the series), Hawks and Bucks were swept aside. In the Finals (a rematch of the 1981 championship match-up), Hakeem Olajuwon's Houston Rockets were no match. A little extra spice was added when the Rockets' Ralph Sampson punched Celtics guard Jerry Sichting in Game 5, but in front of their rabid fans at Boston Garden the result of Game 6 was never in doubt. Building a 28-point lead in the fourth quarter, the Celtics landed their 16th NBA title. It made up for the loss to the Lakers at the same stage the previous season, and the two legendary teams would meet again at the end of the next.

# PLAYING IT STRAIGHT
## LOS ANGELES LAKERS
## 1971-1972

The 1971-72 Lakers not only set a new standard for regular season dominance, winning 69 games (that record would stand for 24 seasons), they also reeled off 33 straight victories, still yet to be topped. For November and December of 1971, they did not taste defeat.

Jerry West, Elgin Baylor, Wilt Chamberlain, Jim McMillian, Gail Goodrich and Happy Hairston are names to bring a smile to the face of a Lakers fan, but the retirement of Baylor nine games into the season could have disrupted them. Instead they went on their 33 game run.

In the Finals, the Lakers let Game 1 slip away, but were untouchable after that. Chamberlain played despite a broken wrist in Game 5 and helped secure the Lakers' first title since moving to Los Angeles. "At that time, I honestly felt that couldn't play, couldn't bend it," Chamberlain later commented. "But with an anti-inflammatory injection and ice packs, it improved." In fact, the injury improved enough for Chamberlain to score 24 points and snag 29 rebounds in Game 5, on his way to the Finals MVP award.

The Celtics' Larry Bird takes a shot during the 1986 NBA Finals matchup against the Rockets

Wilt Chamberlain (left) starred for the Lakers against the Knicks in the Finals

# NBA LEGENDS

## JUST WHAT THE DOCTOR ORDERED
## PHILADELPHIA 76ERS
### 1982–1983

In much the same way that Oscar Robertson found glory late in his career, so Julius Erving was rewarded for his dogged determination in 1983, finally landing that elusive title. The Sixers had come close the previous season, losing in the Finals to the Lakers, but vengeance was sweet in 1983. Philadelphia swept the Lakers to secure the franchise's third NBA championship, and its first in 16 years.

Dr J's star was fading, but he still averaged 21.4 points per game. Teaming up with Andrew Toney and Moses Malone, Philadelphia's potent offense was a handful for any opponent.

Malone, who arrived in a trade before the season, was named league MVP and MVP of the Finals for his efforts in what was to be the only championship season of an illustrious career that saw him elected to the Hall of Fame.

"We did it the long way, and we did it the hard way," Erving commented after the triumph, referencing the many years he had struggled to earn an NBA championship. "But we did it the best way."

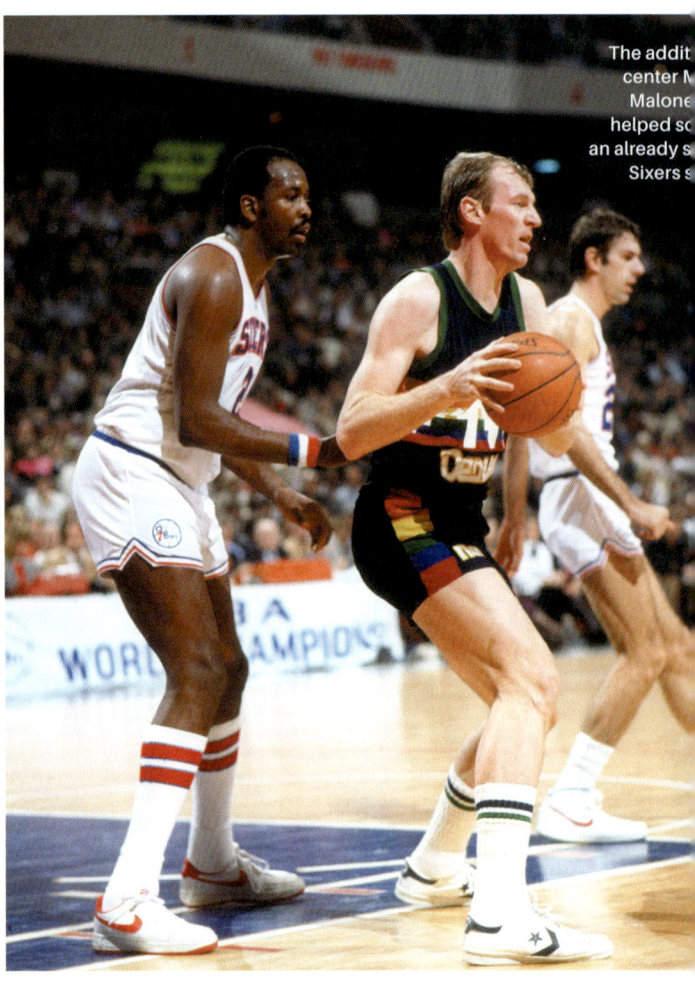

The addition of center Moses Malone helped solidify an already strong Sixers squad.

## A WINNING COMBINATION
## BOSTON CELTICS
### 1964–1965

The Celtics of the late 1950s and 1960s won nine titles in ten seasons, and the 1964-65 team was arguably the best squad of that era. A 62-18 regular season record was the best in team history, and the squad was filled with talent.

Led by Red Auerbach, the Celtics could unleash shooting guard Sam Jones (who averaged 25.9 points per game) and center Bill Russell (24.1 rebounds per game) to smother the opposition. The league was suffering through something of a talent drought at the time, but that did not apply to the Celtics. Five players from the championship team made it into the Hall of Fame – Russell and Sam Jones being joined by KC Jones, Tom Heinsohn and John Havlicek. Whatever the state of affairs in the NBA at the time, winning that many titles, including eight in a row from 1959 to 1966, does not happen by accident.

Guard Sam Jones (24) was inducted to the Hall of Fame in 1984, joining four of his teammates.

## THE UNTOUCHABULLS
## CHICAGO BULLS
## 1991–1992

Jordan was in explosive form throughout the 1991-1992 season

Defending champions always have a target on their backs, but the Bulls of 1991-92 used that to spur them on. They were loaded with talent, headlined by Michael Jordan and Scottie Pippen (averaging 30.1 and 21 points per game, respectively). BJ Armstrong, Horace Grant and Bill Cartwright all played their roles in a season that saw the Bulls get 67 wins, six more than their first title-winning season.

The Bulls had to work harder in the playoffs, being taken to seven games in the Conference Semifinals against the New York Knicks, and six games in both the Conference Finals (versus Cleveland) and the NBA Finals (versus Portland). This was a team where everyone knew their role.

Jordan served notice of his intentions when he sank 35 points in the first half of Game 1, including a scarcely credible six three-pointers. The Trail Blazers were game, but they had no answer to Chicago's triangle offense over the course of the series.

## BACK ON TOP
## LOS ANGELES LAKERS
## 1986–1987

The Lakers' rivalry with the Boston Celtics is the stuff of NBA legend. Three times in the 1980s the two franchises squared off in the NBA Finals. Boston had won in 1984, the Lakers had evened things up the following season, and in 1987 they met again for the third time in four years.

The Lakers were desperate to regain the NBA title following their shocking exit in the Western Conference Finals the year before. In 1986-87, they put everything right.

A team featuring Magic Johnson, James Worthy, Byron Scott and Kareem Abdul-Jabbar was always likely to do well, but the Lakers got solid support from Michael Cooper, Kurt Rambis and AC 'Iron Man' Green.

The team made a key addition in the middle of the season, trading with San Antonio to bring in Mychal Thompson. He was an excellent player, but the Lakers targeted him specifically to take on Boston Celtics forward Kevin McHale. He also offered valuable back-up for Abdul-Jabbar, who was 40 by this time. In the playoffs, the Lakers were imperious, sweeping Denver 3-0, pushing aside Golden State 4-1 and dismantling Seattle 4-0. The rematch with Boston was on.

The NBA Finals all went to the home team, with the exception of Game 4. At the Boston Garden, the Celtics looked set to level the series at two games apiece until Magic Johnson launched the 'baby sky hook' for victory. The win put the Lakers 3-1 up, and they finished the

The champagne erupts in the Lakers locker room following their Finals victory over their bitter rivals

job two games later for a 4-2 triumph.

Lakers coach Pat Riley felt more relief than elation at the victory. Commenting after that tumultuous fourth game of the Finals, he bemoaned how the Lakers' brilliance that season had left them with nothing to celebrate.

"We whipped through the season and playoffs to the point where everyone started talking about being the best ever," he said. "So we were thrust into a no-win situation, in that what we've accomplished is almost joyless." Lakers fans would disagree.

# NBA LEGENDS

# THE KID

## Precocious in Minnesota straight out of high school, Kevin Garnett eventually graduated as a champion in Boston

It was once written that if Prince was Minneapolis's "Commander in chief of culture", then Kevin Garnett was its "Prime minister of cool".

A city buried in the heart of Middle America found its voice when it became one of the epicentres of the music world. In the 1980s and 1990s, star singers and producers of hip hop gathered there to produce beats to which the world could easily dance.

Garnett, spirited there as a teen straight out of high school, discovered the stage to compose sweet music of his own. And in doing so, he reopened doors for those who wanted to bypass college and come directly to the NBA with a genuine hope of making an instant impact.

When the beanpole forward arrived at the Minnesota Timberwolves in 1995 as the fifth pick in the NBA draft and the league's then-youngest-ever player, it felt like a risky gamble for both parties. Until closer inspection at a pre-draft camp, the school kid from Chicago had remained a mystery to most. The Timberwolves, duly impressed, were seduced into making him the first prep-to-pro player in 20 years. And even though his rookie campaign provided inevitable growing pains, doubters would be proved emphatically wrong. An athletic defender and fluid scorer, KG would become one of basketball's greatest power forwards – as well as a Most Valuable Player, an NBA champion and an Olympic champion.

By his second year, he was an All-Star, the first of 15 appearances, as Minnesota claimed a first playoff appearance in the franchise's brief history, fuelled by a young group, including Stephon Marbury and Tom Gugliotta.

The Kid quickly became The Man. Garnett was handed a six-year contract worth $126 million. Ironically, the deal's completion was delayed because he was hanging out at the house of fabled producer Jimmy Jam. "We're listening to Janet (Jackson)'s album," he told his agent. "Could we do it a little later?" He signed on, for huge riches and justified every cent.

Manically intense, Garnett emerged as a supreme intimidator, his savage trash-talking to opponents frequently vicious. But he was most demanding on his own teammates, especially to rookies who had to follow rules or face a ferocious wrath. Chemistry, he claimed, "isn't something that you just throw in the frying pan and mix it up with another something, and throw something on top of that, and then fry it up, put it in a tortilla, put it in the microwave, heat it up and give it to you – and expect it to taste good."

Although the Timberwolves contended, they could not quite carve out a title. Seven successive times, they exited the postseason in the first round. In 2003–04, their superstar claimed the league's MVP award following a 58-24 regular

Garnett was a fierce competitor and an incredibly demanding teammate

# KEVIN GARNETT

*Garnett challenges LeBron James as the Celtics take on the Miami Heat in 2013*

## FROM COURT TO SCREEN

### KEVIN GARNETT'S POST-BASKETBALL CAREER FOLLOWED IN THE FOOTSTEPS OF FELLOW GIANTS IN HOLLYWOOD

Not a bad performance either, playing a version of himself in the 2020 movie *Uncut Gems*. Basketball has so often been at the nexus of the worlds of entertainment and sports. Over the years, NBA stars have regularly made the leap onto the big screen.

Kareem Abdul-Jabbar has a claim to have begun the trend when he appeared in the 1980 comedy *Airplane!* as a super-sized pilot. Then basketball arguably earned its definitive film experience when Michael Jordan and a cast of hoops legends accompanied Bugs Bunny into *Space Jam* in 1996. While Garnett's ex-teammate Ray Allen won plaudits for his role in the Spike Lee drama, *He Got Game*. Others have not fared quite so well. Shaquille O'Neal failed to acquire leading man status for his turns in *Blue Chips* or *Kazaam*. Nevertheless, with the late Kobe Bryant picking up an Oscar for his own documentary and the likes of LeBron James establishing production companies, expect basketballers to keep racking up screen credits.

> "I DON'T HAVE A BARRAGE OF DUNKS. I CAN BARELY JUMP. I'M NOT THAT CREATIVE. I JUST PUT THE BALL THROUGH THE BASKET"

season. In the Western Conference Finals, the LA Lakers prevailed 4-2. Amid Garnett's streak of four rebounding titles, the ceiling could not quite be broken through.

Traded to Boston in July 2007, he acquired running mates in Paul Pierce and Ray Allen – a self-styled Big Three – with the capacity to chase championships, dragging the Celtics to heights unseen since the era of Larry Bird.

Garnett was voted the NBA's Defensive Player of the Year in 2008. His enthusiasm was infectious. "Every time he blocked a shot, he yelled at the top of his lungs," Pierce said. "Every time he dunked, he yelled at the top of his lungs. I'm thinking, 'This guy is crazy'."

A few months later, he screamed at full volume as the Celtics netted their 17th NBA championship, providing 26 points and 14 rebounds in Game 6 of the NBA Finals as the Lakers were thwarted.

It was like facing your fears and fighting back against the school bully, he proclaimed afterwards. "You walk in and as soon as the bully pats your pockets you lay his ass out and you see the expression on his face. You're sorta shook because you know what, you just knocked the bully out and you don't know how he's going to come back. The next morning when you come in and he's not there, it's like a sigh of relief. It's like getting rid of the bully. It's like I knocked the bully's ass out!"

The Celtics would return to the Finals in 2010. This time, the Lakers exacted revenge. Later, he was traded to the Brooklyn Nets before eventually returning to Minnesota for one final season in 2015-16. It concluded a career that saw him become the only NBA player with at least 25,000 points, 10,000 rebounds, 5,000 assists, 1,500 steals and 1,500 blocks. Amid such heroics, he claimed an Olympic gold in Sydney 2000, averaging 10.8 points, and 9.1 rebounds.

Unique to the last, Garnett was content to follow his own path and dance to his own tune.

## KEVIN GARNETT

**POSITION:** Power Forward
**NBA DRAFT:** 1995/Round 1/Pick 5
**CAREER:** Minnesota Timberwolves (1995-2007), Boston Celtics (2007-13), Brooklyn Nets (2013-15), Minnesota Timberwolves (2015-16)

### HIGHLIGHTS:
1x NBA Champion (2008)
1x NBA MVP (2004)
15x NBA All Star (1997, 1998, 2000-11, 2013)
9x All-NBA Team (1999-2005, 2007, 2008)
9x All-Defensive First Team (2000-05, 2008, 2009, 2011)
4x rebounding champion (2004-07)

### STATS:
**REGULAR SEASON**
Points: 26,071 | Rebounds: 14,662 | Assists: 5,445

**PLAYOFFS**
Points: 2,601 | Rebounds: 1,534 | Assists: 471

# SPECIAL DELIVERY

## KARL MALONE WAS NOT ONLY ONE OF THE MOST DOMINATING PLAYERS OF HIS TIME, HE ALSO HAD ONE OF THE GREAT NICKNAMES

Karl Malone got his nickname early. While still at college, playing for Louisiana Tech, a journalist dubbed him 'the Mailman', in recognition of his dependability – the Mailman always delivered, it seemed. But nobody could have imagined quite how dependable he would be after switching to the NBA.

Out of an incredible 19 seasons, in 17 he played in 80 or more games. He played all 82 regular season games ten times, seemingly immune to injury or fatigue.

It was a career twice as long as anyone had a right to expect, so Malone's own explanation for his longevity was uncannily perceptive.

"I look at basketball as 100 per cent physically," he said after announcing his retirement in February 2005, "and 100 per cent mentally. And if I cannot bring you 200 per cent, from me, I cannot bring you anything."

It is usually a cliché to talk of offering 200 per cent, but when your career has lasted 19 seasons, it begins to seem a reasonable claim.

In only one respect could Malone's career be considered anything other than a triumph. He failed to win an NBA title, falling in three Finals, two with the Utah Jazz and one with the LA Lakers. Malone did not duck the question when the time came to look back on his career.

"The thing that will stick with me for the rest of my life is not winning a championship," he admitted. "I am not going to lie to you. That was my ultimate goal, but that was a team goal, not an individual goal."

It was just about the only goal that Malone failed to reach. He was the league MVP on two occasions and a 14-time NBA All-Star. Finishing his career as the second all-time scorer, with nearly 40,000 points, could only be considered a failure by the harshest of critics.

And yet Malone never truly felt at home in the glitz and glamour of the NBA, and questioned his place in the league. At the age of 25, while establishing himself as one of the greatest in the game, he had the humility to ask himself the toughest of questions.

"I'm always thinking, have I paid the price to be here?" he asked. "Have I worked hard enough? Do I deserve to be the Mailman?"

Malone's life did not get off to the easiest start. His father walked out on the family before committing suicide, so taking care of Malone's wellbeing fell to his mother, who worked three jobs to provide for Malone and his eight siblings. Living on a farm in Mount Sinai, his ambitions stretched no further than owning a tractor and trailer of his own.

At Summerfield High School, in Louisiana, he led his team to three straight Class C State Championships and was recruited heavily by an up-and-coming University of Arkansas.

Malone's mother did not think he had the academic ability to succeed at such a big school and insisted that he stay

Malone (right) and John Stockton formed a formidable partnership during their time together in Utah

## KARL MALONE | 129

Immense physical strength allowed Malone to dominate opposing defenses

### KARL MALONE

**POSITION:** Power Forward
**NBA DRAFT:** 1985/Round 1/Pick 13
**CAREER:** Utah Jazz (1985-2003), LA Lakers (2003-2004)

••••

**HIGHLIGHTS:**
2 x NBA MVP (1997, 1999),
14 x NBA All-Star (1988-98, 2000-02)
14x All-NBA Team (1988-2001)
3x All-Defensive First Team (1997-99)

**STATS:**
**REGULAR SEASON**
Points: 36,928 | Assists: 5,248 | Rebounds: 14,968

**PLAYOFFS**
Points: 4,761 | Assists: 610 | Rebounds: 2,062

# NBA LEGENDS

local. Andy Russo, basketball coach at Louisiana Tech, could scarcely believe his ears when Malone's mother called to confirm that the high-school phenomenon would be playing for his Bulldogs.

Malone's academic struggles cost him his first season at college, but in his sophomore year he had lifted his grades sufficiently to play. His physical prowess had never been in question.

"He was the fastest and strongest guy we had," said Russo. "During the first practice he broke a backboard and when we worked out, he broke a machine in the weight room."

Malone led the Bulldogs to the NCAA tournament for the first time in their history in his second season playing at Tech, duplicating the feat in his third and final season.

Though already able to hold his own physically against the big men of the NBA, Malone's draft stock was weakened by a belief that his college performances had declined over his career. There was also a perception that he was simply too 'nice'.

Expecting to be drafted by the Dallas Mavericks with the eighth pick (he had already acquired an apartment in Dallas), Malone found himself sitting and waiting until the 13th selection, when the Utah Jazz grabbed him. He was to prove the steal of the draft.

Malone got off to a slow start in his professional career, but on 4 December 1985 he arrived, scoring 25 points against the LA Lakers. He made the All-Rookie Team and began to make big strides in his second season.

Big scores began to flow from January 1987, with totals of 38, 36 and 38 again. Between March and April he hit the 30-point mark no fewer than six times. He was already an emerging superstar, but his big games often ended in losses. He needed help.

The following season he got it, with the emergence of John Stockton at point guard. Stockton had been drafted the year before Malone, but had developed more slowly. In the 1987–1988 season the two began a lethal partnership, executing a pick-and-roll offense that few could live with.

As well as the two men complemented each other, even more remarkable was the fact that Stockton would prove every bit as durable as Malone, continuing to play till the age of 40. The NBA would have reason to fear the dynamic pairing for years to come.

But although Malone's career became one of repeated All-Star appearances, it was also marked by repeated failures in the playoffs. Nine times his team crashed out of the playoffs in the first round.

Amid the playoff heartache,

Malone stands next to Stockton to receive his 1996 Olympic gold medal

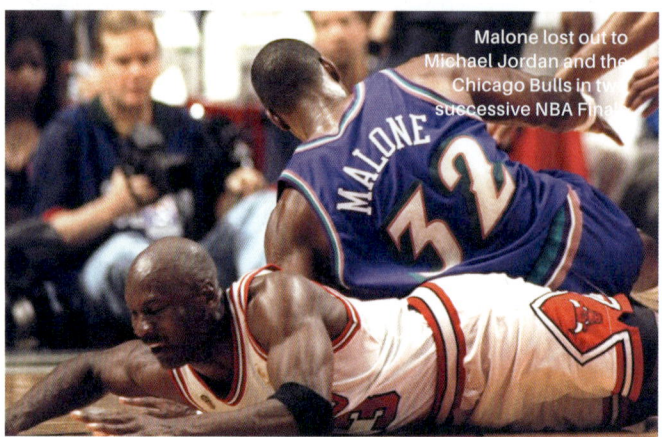
Malone lost out to Michael Jordan and the Chicago Bulls in two successive NBA Finals

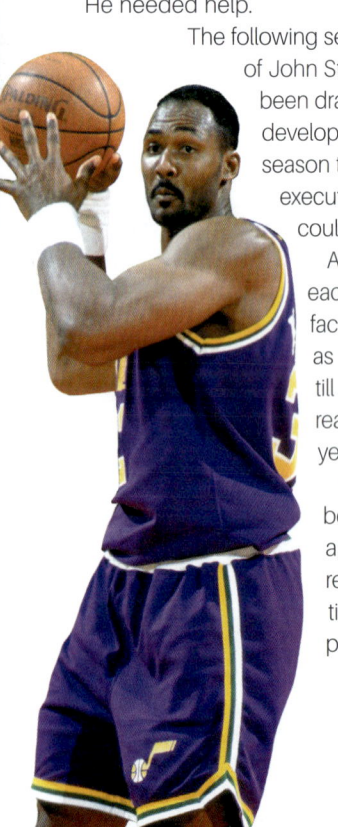

however, Malone's consistency was reaching legendary proportions. The 1989–1990 season saw him open with 20 consecutive 20-point games. Playing in all 82 games that season, he finished with an average of 31 points per game, the highest mark of his career.

Malone's incredible durability was noted by foes and teammates alike. It was too remarkable to miss.

Playoff success followed, with the Jazz making Conference Finals in 1992, 1994 and 1996, but all three series ended in defeat and Malone had to be content with success of a different kind – he won gold medals at the Barcelona and Atlanta Olympic Games.

After his second gold medal, the ultimate prizes in basketball suddenly came within reach. Averaging 27.4 points and 9.9 rebounds per game, Malone became the oldest first-time winner of the league MVP award in 1997 and his play helped lift the Jazz to a franchise record 64 wins.

As he also made the All-Defensive Team, there was little doubt that he was a dominating force at the peak of his powers. Utah beat the Houston Rockets to advance to the NBA Finals for the first time.

Malone had tasted the ultimate in personal glory, but team success remained elusive. The suffocating Chicago Bulls defense, led by Dennis Rodman, was too much to overcome and the Jazz lost the Finals in six games. Despite Malone's best efforts, the following season ended in exactly the same manner.

There was hope in 1998, when Michael Jordan's retirement

*Malone (no 32) in action for Louisiana Tech*

## KARL MALONE

### GETTING PHYSICAL

#### MALONE HAD GREAT STRENGTH, BUT HOURS IN THE GYM TOOK HIM TO THE NEXT LEVEL

Malone was often compared to a bodybuilder thanks to his chiselled physique. Standing 6-feet 9-inches tall and weighing 256 pounds in his prime, he was always one of the most imposing men on the court, but he had worked hard to attain that physicality.

His strength was initially developed through farm work, including wrestling razorback hogs in order to put rings through their noses. As well as being 'farm strong', however, Malone found that he also enjoyed working out in the gym, and he gradually developed from a tall, skinny kid to a physically imposing giant.

Once in the NBA, he refused to slow down and developed a punishing workout routine that honed speed, endurance and strength. He would run a hundred metres ten times, following up with three 200-metre runs and then three 300-metre efforts.

Switching to weights, he would perform bicep curls with 60 pounds, and bench press 270. "I like doing it," he insisted when questioned about his work ethic. "I see myself improving. I feel the power and strength growing."

Others saw it too. "I've never seen Karl tired," said his long-time partner in crime John Stockton. "He's on a different standard than the rest of us."

*Intense sessions in the gym helped Malone sculpt his bodybuilder's physique*

> "ALTHOUGH MALONE'S CAREER BECAME ONE OF REPEATED ALL-STAR APPEARANCES, IT WAS ALSO MARKED BY REPEATED FAILURES IN THE PLAYOFFS"

and the shortening of the season to just 50 games due to strike action promised to be the perfect boost for the ageing star. Malone earned his second MVP award, but a second-round playoff exit proved the Jazz were on the decline. A second-round series defeat in 2000 was followed by three consecutive first-round failures, meaning Malone's career with the Jazz ended just as it had begun.

Malone had given everything to his team, but at the age of 39 he was almost finished. Stockton retired after the 2002–2003 season, at the age of 40, and Malone allowed himself one last shot at glory. As a free agent, he joined the LA Lakers in search of a championship, but fell in the Finals once more.

Malone's incredible journey was at an end, but he had been a towering presence in the league for an incredible 19 seasons, and although he had faded slightly towards the end (he suffered the first serious injuries of his career while with the Lakers and played in just 42 games in his final season), he would be remembered as the durable, reliable Mailman, who always delivered.

"He runs the court like a small man," commented Golden State Warriors coach Don Nelson at the height of Malone's career, "then overpowers bigger people. Is there a more dominant power forward in the game today?

"If there is, I'd like to see him."

*Malone in an unfamiliar shirt and unfamiliar number in his final season*